Skylab
Pioneer Space Station

Rand McNally & Company *Chicago • New York • San Francisco*

Skylab
Pioneer Space Station

By William G. Holder and William D. Siuru, Jr.
Introduction by Wernher Von Braun

To Ruthann and Nancy

Library of Congress Cataloging in Publication Data

Holder, William G.   1937–
  Skylab: pioneer space station.

    SUMMARY: Follows the progress of the Skylab
project from the preliminary planning and construction
of the laboratory through the experiments, launches,
and experiences of the nine astronauts living and
working in earth orbit.
    1. Skylab project—Juvenile literature.
[1. Skylab project. 2. Space stations] I. Siuru,
William D., joint author. II. Title.
TL789.8.U6S556   629.44′5   74-2484
ISBN 0-528-82556-9
ISBN 0-528-82557-7 (lib. bdg.)

Introduction

With the orbiting of Skylab, the United States took an important and significant step in the application of two decades of space research and technology and extended study of Earth, Sun, and intergalactic space. This space station permitted us to study the long-term effects of the space environment on man himself and his capability to perform a variety of scientific and technological tasks out there. During the Skylab mission, nine astronauts spent some 171 days monitoring or conducting more than 270 experiments in many areas.

Skylab provided us with our first large, stable platform in space from which man could observe and actively study the changing environment of large areas of our planet. Since Skylab orbited over the same location every five days, the astronauts could intensively study changes during this interval in meteorological, hydrological, geological, and agricultural conditions. Because the space station swept over some 147,705,000 square miles of the surface of the Earth, between 50° north and 50° south latitude, these studies concerned and directly affected the well-being and life of some 90 percent of the world's 3,800,000,000 people.

At the same time, the largest array of solar research instruments ever developed was probing the Sun's physics and chemistry from Skylab's unique vantage point far above the radiation-filtering effects of the Earth's atmosphere, which prevents such study from the Earth's surface. Other instruments, including one developed by scientists in France, were surveying the Milky Way star field and recording data for a better understanding of the physics of the interplanetary medium as well.

With Skylab, we had a manned space station that utilized the technology of the past, studied the present, and looked to the future. From the knowledge we gained of the Earth's resources and environment, we are in a better position to improve the lot of all men. With the knowledge we gained of how well man performed in space over long periods of time and how he adjusted to life in medium-sized space stations, we can begin designing larger and permanent space station complexes—accommodating tens and later hundreds of people, cities in the sky—that will someday circle the Earth, extending man's knowledge of Earth, universe, and self.

WERNHER VON BRAUN

Germantown, MD.
April 1973

Contents

The delayed launch of the Saturn IB carrying the first crew into space to man the orbiting Skylab took place at 9:00 A.M. on May 25, 1973. Commander Charles Conrad, Jr., Science Pilot Joseph P. Kerwin, and Pilot Paul J. Weitz—known as the "Fix Anything" crew—repeatedly proved their ability to cope with the unexpected. Without their determination and occasionally ingenious handling of unforeseen problems, the entire Skylab mission might have been scrubbed.

Why Skylab?

1

The large countdown clock in front of the reviewing stand at Cape Kennedy told the story. It was May 14, 1973, and fleeting seconds were slipping away before what well might be the last launch of the Saturn V moon rocket. But this Saturn V was unique. It was not carrying a trio of astronauts to the moon as its predecessors had done; no men were aboard. Poised like a pencil on Pad A of Launch Complex 39, liquid oxygen venting from its sides, the giant rocket was preparing to write an epic chapter in the space history of the United States. For the objective of this Saturn V was to place Skylab, America's pioneer space station, in orbit around the earth. If all went well, on the following day a three-man crew would be launched from neighboring Launch Pad 39B to rendezvous, dock, enter the space station, and man it for 28 days.

Thirty seconds remained. The massive launch vehicle was switched onto its own power. "T minus twelve seconds, eleven, ten, nine, eight." At T minus 7 the public address system blared: "Ignition sequence started." The liquid oxygen and rocket fuel were brought together and ignited. A bright splash of orange burst from the vehicle's base and almost instantaneously exploded outward into a massive boiling circle of flame. The service arms of the gantry retracted, and for an instant the vehicle stood alone as though undecided whether or not to start its upward climb. The bonds of earth shackled it.

Then slowly, almost agonizingly, the six-million-pound beast began its climb. The billowing circle of flame at its base gathered in beneath the rocket as the five thundering engines pushed it upward. Hundreds of tons of complex equipment rode atop a spout of yellow-white flame hundreds of feet long.

The power generated by more than 7½-million pounds of thrust awed both eye and ear. Had there ever been such a conflagration! The flames changed from red to orange to palest yellow as heat—and thrust—increased. Sound waves from what was perhaps one of the loudest noises ever produced by man buffeted the flat Florida countryside. Shuddering shock waves followed.

Skylab rode above the flame, proudly erect, rapidly picking up speed, cutting upward through a low-hanging cloud, reappearing. Too quickly, then, it disappeared into the low sky. Only its thunderous voice remained, now receding, and the pall of black smoke that churned around the vacant launch site.

Skylab was on its way.

Among watchers at Cape Kennedy and ground controllers at Houston, exhilaration at what appeared to be a clean launch was quickly extinguished. Sixty-three seconds into the flight, NASA ground controllers had indications of trouble, and an hour later the scope of the problem began to take shape. With the stresses of launch, Skylab's heat and micrometeoroid shield had been stripped away, one of the solar power wings on the Orbital Workshop had been torn off, and the second solar power wing was jammed in a nearly closed position. Lacking full thermal protection, exposed to the intense rays of the sun, temperatures began to rise in the space station. Without the electricity produced from the Orbital Workshop's solar power wings, Skylab was receiving too little power from the solar power wings on the Apollo Telescope Mount to permit full functioning of the workshop's air-conditioning system.

In the hours that followed the launch, heat rose to dangerous levels inside the station, threatening delicate electronic equipment and causing concern that the atmosphere in the Orbital Workshop was being poisoned. Source of the deadly gas, it was suspected, was the station's urethane insulation; heated beyond its tolerance, it was breaking down and giving off deadly fumes. Certainly the manned launch planned for the following day would be postponed. Possibly the entire mission would have to be aborted. Faced with that sobering thought, engineers and technicians all over the country rolled up their sleeves and went to work. This, then, was Skylab on its first day in orbit. And this book is the story of the Skylab mission—its development, its equipment, its astronauts, and finally and most important of all, its reason for being.

Why Space Stations?

It had taken almost a decade, some $25 billion, and the efforts of thousands of people to place Apollo astronauts Neil Armstrong and Edwin "Buzz" Aldrin on the moon. For his investment in the Apollo program, the American taxpayer was rewarded with far more than a few pounds of lunar rocks, new ways of packaging orange juice, and computer systems for use in medical research. There were the visible fruits of the Apollo program: the hardware and the facilities. And there was a large pool of trained engineers and technicians capable of solving not only problems in space, but problems of equal seriousness right here on earth. While the Apollo program moved along on course, some of these men turned their attention to the earth and the use of space within a few thousand miles of the earth's surface. The reasoning went something like this.

If significant information could be obtained from unmanned satellites—which had for some time been used in weather forecasting and for transmitting radio and TV signals—could not even more information be had from satellites with men in them, operating at an altitude of several hundred miles? With men aboard, cameras could be more accurately aimed, space experiments could be conducted, repairs could if necessary be made on delicate equipment, and an all-around better understanding could be arrived at of man in space, the planet earth, and the sun.

From his new and lofty perch, man could keep track of land and water usage, could predict floods and droughts and even tell where to build dams to prevent both. He could provide early warning of approaching tornadoes and hurricanes, could discover forest fires before they raged out of control, could help detect forest- and crop-killing diseases, and could find petroleum and mineral deposits even in the most inaccessible parts of the world. He could spot sources of polluted air and water and actually see how pollutants are spread by wind and water currents, perhaps leading to solutions to the problems of filth and litter. He could even guide fishermen to good fishing spots and study the migration of wild animals.

And that could well be just the beginning.

Manned space stations could someday become control towers in orbit, directing travel on the oceans and airways. Space-station crews could detect icebergs and fogbanks and locate lost ships and planes. A space station could be the starting point for journeys to other planets or to the moon. It could be a parking place for "space tugs" used to rescue people lost in space or to carry repair crews to disabled satellites. A space station could utilize the abundance of solar energy found in the cold, quiet weightlessness of space to power space factories capable of producing new materials not available from earthbound factories.

The real value of manned satellites is only beginning to be understood. As man actually lives and works in space, innumerable and as yet undreamed-of ways to utilize space stations will be discovered.

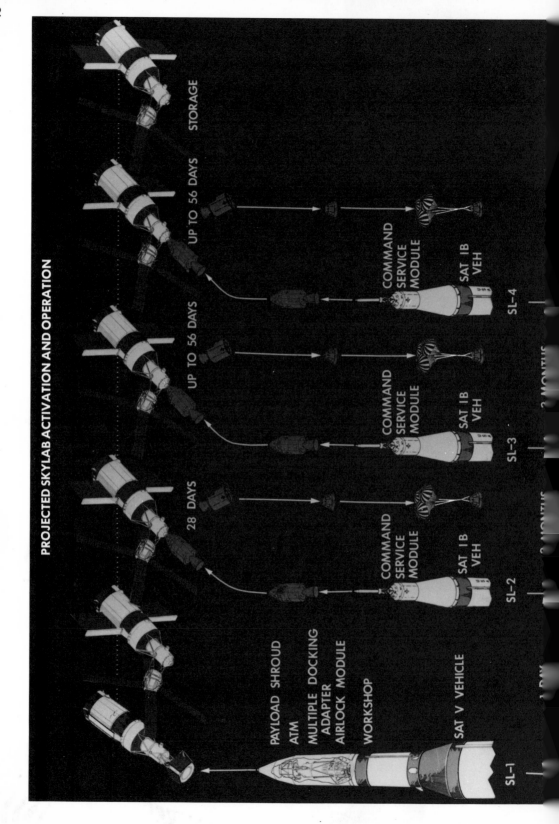

PROJECTED SKYLAB ACTIVATION AND OPERATION

STORAGE

UP TO 56 DAYS

UP TO 56 DAYS

28 DAYS

PAYLOAD SHROUD
ATM
MULTIPLE DOCKING ADAPTER
AIRLOCK MODULE
WORKSHOP

COMMAND SERVICE MODULE

COMMAND SERVICE MODULE

COMMAND SERVICE MODULE

SAT 1B VEH

SAT 1B VEH

SAT 1B VEH

SL–4

SL–3

SL–2

SAT V VEHICLE

SL–1

Skylab As Planned

The original Skylab flight program called for an eight-month-long life in orbit of the space station, with three separately launched three-man crews living aboard the orbiting craft for a total of 140 days.

The unmanned space station—consisting of the Orbital Workshop, the Apollo Telescope Mount, the Airlock Module, and the Multiple Docking Adapter—would be placed in orbit by the Saturn V, the moon rocket, at a height of 235 nautical miles, crossing the equator at an angle of about 50 degrees. This would be called Skylab 1.

Approximately 24 hours after this first launch, a smaller rocket, the Saturn IB, would leave the bonds of earth carrying the first three-man crew in an Apollo Command/Service Module. This second launch would be labeled Skylab 2, or SL-2. The Saturn would place its payload into an 81-by-120-nautical-mile orbit, from which the engine aboard the Command/Service Module would then boost the spacecraft to the 235-nautical-mile orbit of Skylab. The men would enter the space station and remain aboard for 28 days, during which time a single space walk would take place on the 26th day to retrieve film from the Apollo Telescope Mount and to reload the cameras with fresh film. The crew would then prepare the space station for a period of emptiness and would return to earth.

The second Command/Service Module—identified as Skylab 3, or SL-3—would be placed in orbit some 50 days later. This three-man crew would occupy the space station for a 56-day period before returning to earth. Following a dormancy period of from 30 to 40 days, the third crew—in a launch identified as Skylab 4, or SL-4—would go aloft and remain in the space station for 56 days. With the return to earth of this last crew, the Skylab mission would be completed.

The flight plan was sound, but adjustments in the time schedule became necessary following the troublesome launch of the space station. Launch of the first crew had to be delayed for 10 days while ground crews worked frantically to devise tools, equipment, and techniques for repairing the giant space station. The first crew performed more extravehicular activities than planned. The second crew's occupancy of the workshop was extended from 56 to 59 days and the third crew's from 56 to 84 days. Additional adaptations occurred during the course of the program as circumstances dictated. While nobody would have chosen to build problems into Skylab's original plan, the various shifts and changes did demonstrate the remarkable flexibility of the astronauts and the ground crews when faced with the unexpected.

Skylab, in its many months in orbit, went a long way toward proving to doubters the importance of man himself in space. Glitch after glitch was solved because men were there to make corrections.

Each of the three Skylab crews had its own emblem. The first crew's patch shows the giant orbiting laboratory silhouetted against the earth, which in turn blocks the light of the sun— a solar eclipse visible only from space, witnessed by only a handful of men.

The three main objectives of the Skylab program are illustrated on the second manned mission's emblem. Studies of man himself are symbolized by the central human figure adapted from a drawing by Leonardo da Vinci. Studies of the sun and of the earth's resources are represented by the red and blue hemispheres.

A tree, representing man's natural environment; a hydrogen atom, the basic building block of the universe; a human figure embraced by a rainbow extending to the tree and the atom— these are the symbols on the emblem of the third manned Skylab mission. They express man's wish to direct technology with wisdom and regard for his natural environment.

The Goals of Skylab

As conceived by its planners, the goals of the Skylab program were threefold: the study of the sun and stars, applications of manned spaceflight as they might affect the earth, and increased knowledge about the effects on men of long-duration space missions. Space studies would contribute to the existing body of knowledge of the sun and stars. Applications of manned spaceflight would include experiments that could lead to new and expanded information about agriculture and forestry; rivers, lakes, and oceans; mineral resources; and the earth's environment. And, in their several-month-long stays aboard Skylab, the crews were to evaluate the long-term effects of weightlessness on bones, muscles, blood, and cells.

With so many possibilities for investigation, engineers designed the space station to make possible a diverse selection of experiments. In all, more than 270 individual experiments were planned for the Skylab program, with everyday living itself possibly the most important of all.

Skylab would help find answers to problems here on earth, and it would provide information leading to space stations of the future.

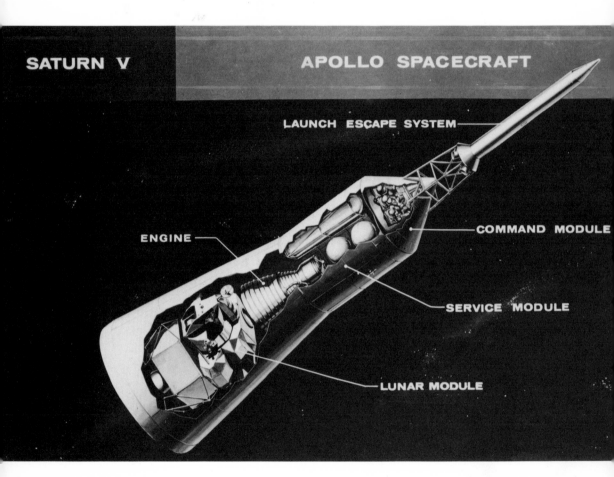

SATURN V

APOLLO SPACECRAFT

LAUNCH ESCAPE SYSTEM

ENGINE

COMMAND MODULE

SERVICE MODULE

LUNAR MODULE

Skylab's Beginnings

With the suborbital flight of Alan Shepard in 1961 and the orbital flight of John Glenn in 1962, the United States made its debut in space. These historic Mercury flights, spectacular in their day, showed that man could indeed withstand the rigors of launch and travel in orbit and demonstrated fundamental techniques of spaceflight. But it was not until the Gemini flights of 1965 and 1966 that the principles and procedures applicable to orbital space stations of the future were actually developed.

Rendezvous and docking techniques had to be perfected in order to join two spacecrafts so that crews could be exchanged and stations re-supplied. Rendezvous was accomplished on Gemini 6 and 7, and docking was first demonstrated on Gemini 8 when Neil Armstrong and David Scott linked their capsule to an unmanned Agena spacecraft.

During the course of the Gemini program, other vital objectives were achieved. Frank Borman and Jim Lovell stayed in orbit an unprecedented 331 hours during Gemini 7, a record not surpassed until 1970 when the Russian crew of Soyuz 9 remained in orbit 425 hours. On Gemini 4, Ed White walked in space, as did Gene Cernan on Gemini 9, Mike Collins on Gemini 10, Richard Gordon on Gemini 11, and Buzz Aldrin on Gemini 12. These space walks helped perfect extravehicular-activity techniques that would be useful in the future.

Experiments involving eating, sleeping, and exercising in space were conducted on the Gemini flights. And extensive photographs of the earth's surface were taken, giving us our first indications of the value of manned space satellites in mapping the earth and in monitoring natural resources.

By the mid-sixties, the United States possessed hardware that could be mated into a space station, had personnel experienced in living and working in space for extended periods of time, and was well along toward a developed set of procedures for surviving and doing useful work there. And meanwhile, space engineers were quietly thinking of the future, planning stations with 10-, 30-, and even 100-man crews and with lifetime in orbit measured in years. Abbreviations like MORL, for Manned Orbiting Research Laboratory; MOSS, for Manned Orbiting Space Station; and LORL, for Large Orbital Research Laboratory, were just a few of the names bantered about the aerospace industry. Every space contractor worth his salt had a pet space-station scheme, some the mere dreams of engineers, others detailed studies sponsored and paid for by NASA and the U.S. Air Force. One such project that almost made it to the launch pad was the Air Force's Manned Orbiting Laboratory, MOL in aerospace language.

The Manned Orbiting Laboratory

The MOL program was initiated by the Air Force in 1965 and had as its objective a two-man space station in which astronauts could remain in orbit for up to a month. The purpose of the MOL was to see if man could live and function in the space environment for extended periods—a goal consistent with the later Skylab's goals.

The MOL had two main parts, which when joined gave it the look of a giant Thermos bottle. From launch to orbit and on the return trip to earth, the astronauts were to have ridden in the same two-man Gemini capsule used so successfully by NASA in 1965 and 1966. Behind the Gemini was the laboratory itself, a ten-foot-diameter cylinder roughly the size of a large house trailer, in which were located living quarters for the crew and all the apparatus for the experiments they were to perform. The entire MOL—Gemini capsule, laboratory, and astronauts—was to have been launched into orbit atop the Titan IIIM space booster. The design of the Titan IIIM was based on the Titan II Intercontinental Ballistic Missile (ICBM), but greatly modified to launch the 30,000-pound MOL into space. The Titan IIIM, with its MOL payload, was to have been launched from a specially built launch complex at Vandenburg Air Force Base in California.

Unfortunately, the MOL program was never completed. In 1969, after much rescheduling, many delays, and several extensions, the program was canceled, a victim of decreased defense budgets and the increased cost of the war in Vietnam. Had the MOL been completed on schedule, the Air Force would have had the world's first space station.

Apollo Extension Systems

While the MOL program was being pursued by the Air Force, NASA was examining various plans for use of the Apollo lunar hardware in a variety of space-station applications. These NASA studies, initially

Above left, America's first manned spacecraft. The Mercury space capsule, Freedom 7, carried Alan Shepard on his famous suborbital flight in 1961.

Above right, Gemini 6 and 7 are shown in orbit. Astronauts Walter M. Schirra, Jr., and Thomas P. Stafford maneuvered their Gemini space capsule to within one foot of the Gemini 7 occupied by Frank Borman and James A. Lovell, Jr.

given the names Apollo X and Apollo Extension Studies, considered using just about every piece of Apollo hardware in one way or another.

The simplest plan called for use of only the Command/Service Module, which already had all the essential features of an orbiting station. The module would be used many times with three-man crews and would stay in space up to 14 days. For a longer mission, the crew's living space would have had to be increased. This could have been done by removing one crew member and much of the equipment designed specifically for lunar use, resulting in almost 200 cubic feet of additional living space. Some 5,000 pounds of experimental gear would have been housed in the unpressurized Service Module. However, this space-station concept never reached the metal-cutting stage.

Another space-station concept again made use of the Command/Service Module, this time with the Spacecraft-Lunar Module Adapter which protected the Lunar Module during Apollo's acceleration and ascent through the earth's atmosphere. In this scheme the adapter

The U.S. Air Force's never-to-be-completed Manned Orbiting Laboratory, the MOL. The large, white section is the laboratory itself. The black conical section is the Gemini capsule.

would have been turned into a 5,600-cubic-foot space laboratory, with plenty of room for crew quarters and for many space experiments. NASA planned this station, with a useful life of more than a year, for as many as six astronauts. Three astronauts riding in the Command Module would have been launched with the station. After reaching orbit, the Command/Service Module would have been turned around so that the crew could have crawled through the tunnel in the Command Module's nose and into the space laboratory in the adapter. Shortly thereafter, another Command/Service Module, carrying three more astronauts, would have docked at the other end of the laboratory, bringing the station's crew size to six. Every three months a Command/Service Module would have brought new crews and supplies to the laboratory. This plan, too, was never put into operation.

Many of the interesting ideas for space stations based on Apollo hardware made use of the Lunar Module. In some schemes, the Lunar Module, stripped of most of its original gear, housed telescopes and various experiments. Several designs made provisions for overcoming the possible effects of prolonged weightlessness. In one concept the Command/Service Module and the Lunar Module were to have been linked by over 200 feet of steel cables. The two parts of this interesting space station would have rotated at about three revolutions per minute around a center located between the two objects. This three-revolutions-per-minute rotation would have produced in the Lunar Module laboratory a one-g gravity like that on earth. The Command/Service Module, however, would have had a gravitational pull equal to only one-fourth that of the laboratory.

In still another concept, a one-man centrifuge located just behind the Lunar Module could have been used routinely by the crew to avoid the effects of prolonged zero-gravity living.

Interestingly, the Lunar Module, a complex and sophisticated piece of space hardware, was the only major component of the Apollo hardware not used in Skylab.

Another Apollo extension project was the Wet Workshop. In this concept, the Saturn IVB, one of the Saturn V rocket stages not only was to have been the main portion of the space station but was also to have functioned as a regular rocket stage in getting itself into orbit. As a rocket stage at lift-off, its tanks would have held supercold liquid oxygen and liquid hydrogen, the two propellants in their respective tanks separated by a large, curved common bulkhead. The liquid hydrogen would have been carried in the upper tank, while the lower tank would have held the liquid oxygen. Once the S-IVB reached its orbit, its rocket propellants used up, the astronauts were to have assembled all the gear inside it necessary to change it from an empty rocket stage to a working space station. The gear would have been

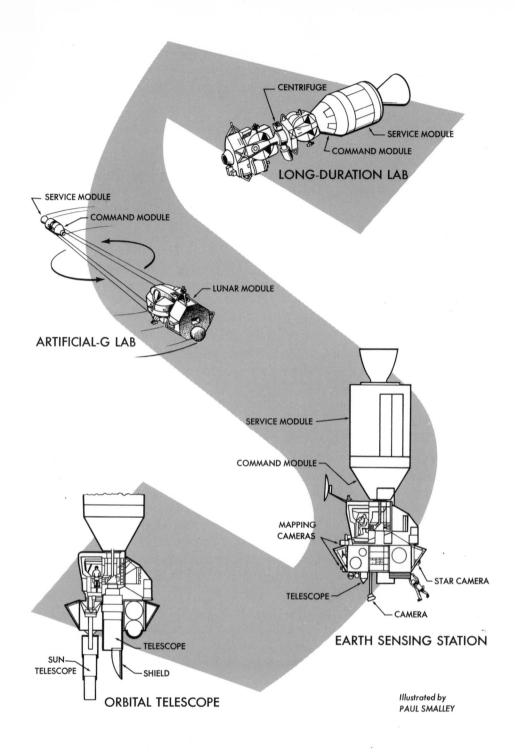

CENTRIFUGE

SERVICE MODULE

COMMAND MODULE

LONG-DURATION LAB

SERVICE MODULE

COMMAND MODULE

LUNAR MODULE

ARTIFICIAL-G LAB

SERVICE MODULE

COMMAND MODULE

MAPPING CAMERAS

STAR CAMERA

TELESCOPE

CAMERA

EARTH SENSING STATION

TELESCOPE

SUN TELESCOPE

SHIELD

ORBITAL TELESCOPE

Illustrated by
PAUL SMALLEY

APOLLO X AND EXTENDED APOLLO CONCEPTS

stored in the Multiple Docking Adapter during launch.

As with the current Skylab, the crew would have been launched by a Saturn IB. However, the Wet Workshop concept differed from Skylab, in that, because the S-IVB was to have done part of the job of getting to orbit, the smaller Saturn IB (of which the S-IVB was the second stage) rather than a Saturn V could have been used for placement of the laboratory in space. A further difference between the Wet Workshop and Skylab concepts was in the handling of the Apollo Telescope Mount. It would not have been launched with the space station but would have been sent up at a later date by another Saturn IB. Like the Command/Service Module, it would have rendezvoused and docked with the space station. The Wet Workshop was an interesting approach to a space station. It, too, was not to be, but it did lay much of the groundwork for Skylab.

In July 1969 NASA decided to change to the current Skylab program, using the massive Saturn V to place the space station in orbit. With the gigantic lifting capability of the Saturn V, the completely outfitted Skylab, including the Apollo Telescope Mount, could be placed in orbit with a single launch. This plan eliminated a great deal of work by the astronauts in getting the station ready for living and working. It also eliminated much tricky maneuvering in linking the Apollo Telescope Mount with the station. Because the Saturn IVB was converted for use as the Orbital Workshop, the current Skylab concept is often referred to as the Dry Workshop as opposed to the earlier Wet Workshop designation.

Apollo Flight and Hardware

The basic idea behind Skylab—which originally had the less catchy but more descriptive name of the Apollo Applications Program—was to make use of equipment, techniques, and facilities from the Apollo lunar program to build America's first space station. That being the case, what did NASA engineers have to work with?

They had a pool of experience. Astronauts, engineers, and technicians had had the opportunity to become thoroughly familiar with the Apollo hardware, much of which would be used with Skylab. Even troubles like those that clouded the flight of Apollo 13—when it looked as though astronauts Jim Lovell, Fred Haise, and John Swigert might not make it back to earth but did in a seemingly miraculous recovery of the mission—helped in a way to prepare the NASA contractor team for the emergencies that were later to beset Skylab.

NASA engineers had the gigantic three-stage Saturn V launch vehicle, which could place a payload of over 214,000 pounds into earth orbit, along with the massive Launch Complex 39 at the John F.

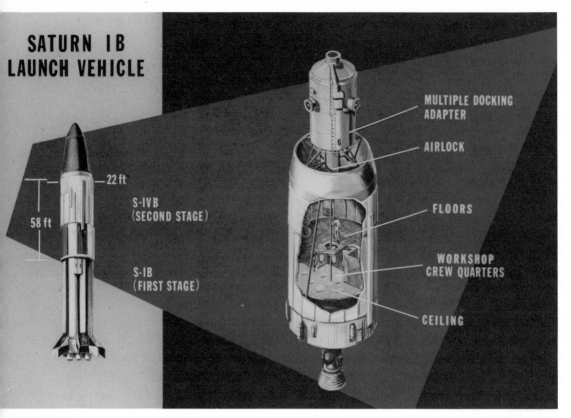

SATURN IB
LAUNCH VEHICLE

22 ft

58 ft

S-IVB
(SECOND STAGE)

S-IB
(FIRST STAGE)

MULTIPLE DOCKING
ADAPTER

AIRLOCK

FLOORS

WORKSHOP
CREW QUARTERS

CEILING

A concept that preceded Skylab, the Wet Workshop. Fuel filled, the workshop was to have functioned as a rocket stage during launch. In orbit, its
fuel expended, the workshop was to have been outfitted to become part of a
space station.

Kennedy Space Center, Cape Kennedy, Florida, where the Saturn V
could be assembled and launched.

They had the smaller two-stage Saturn IB, which was built to test
the Apollo lunar hardware and could place about 40,000 pounds into
earth orbit. In one launch of the Saturn IB, the third stage of the
Saturn V had been tested. In another, the Lunar Module had been
tested in a 100-mile-high orbit. Its most famous test flight occurred on
October 11, 1968, when it launched astronauts Walter Cunningham,
Donn Eisele, and Walter Schirra for an almost-11-day orbit. The
Saturn IB had been launched only five times, the last time in 1968.
NASA had purchased several extra Saturn IBs and stored them for the
day they would be used in the Skylab program.

The jewel of the entire Apollo program—and it was this that most interested the engineers—was the Apollo spacecraft itself, made up of the Command/Service Module, the Lunar Module, the Spacecraft-Lunar Module Adapter, and the Launch Escape System.

The cone-shaped Command Module, really a small space station in itself, provided living and working quarters for the Apollo crews during the typical 200-plus-hour Apollo lunar missions. The cramped cabin provided a mere 210 cubic feet of living area, about as much space as found in the family station wagon. Here the three-man crews ate, slept, worked, and did all the other things needed to get safely to and from the moon.

All the controls and displays needed to operate and navigate the Apollo spacecraft were located in the Command Module, as well as the systems that kept the crews comfortable, a maze of electronic gear for communicating with the earth and with the two astronauts when they explored the moon, and TV equipment for sending pictures and scientific data back to earth. At the base of the Command Module was a heat shield to allow the capsule to return to the earth without burning up in the earth's atmosphere. And finally, stored in the apex, were three large parachutes for deployment just prior to touchdown in the Pacific Ocean to cushion the arrival of the capsule on earth.

Behind the Command Module was the large Service Module, aptly named because it provided most of the essential services for the Apollo spacecraft. Inside were fuel cells and batteries to supply electrical power, tanks of oxygen for breathing, tanks of hydrogen and oxygen for the fuel cells, and a highly efficient cooling system.

At the rear of the Service Module was a rocket engine used to place the Apollo into orbit around the moon and finally to blast it back toward the earth when the moon venture was finished. Tanks inside the Service Module held propellants for this rocket engine and for the other small attitude-control engines mounted on the outside. Since for most of the lunar journeys, the Command and Service Modules were joined, the two were usually called the Command/Service Module. Only in the final minutes before splashdown were they separated.

Between the Service Module and the Saturn V's upper stage was the Lunar Module, shrouded within the Spacecraft-Lunar Module Adapter. Much has been written of the Lunar Module, which need not be included here since it was omitted from the Skylab concept. Let it simply be said that the Lunar Module was a highly efficient, totally functional marvel of space equipment that performed admirably in placing men on the moon and returning them to the waiting spacecraft.

As carefully designed and tested as every other element of the Apollo spacecraft—but fortunately never put into operation—was the Launch Escape System, mounted above the Command Module and consisting of a trusswork tower joined to a rocket-powered missile. In an emergency on the pad or during the first three minutes into launch, the Launch Escape System could be activated either by the Instrument Unit or by the astronauts themselves. The powerful rocket motor was capable of creating nearly 150,000 pounds of thrust for three seconds—just long enough to lift the Command Module and its occupants to an altitude over the ocean where the Command Module's parachutes could deploy and lower it safely to earth. The Launch Escape System was jettisoned when the Command/Service Module reached an altitude of 140,000 feet, a height at which the spacecraft could make its own descent if necessary.

This, then, was what Apollo was all about. The hardware gave engineers who were thinking of space stations a lot with which to work. Many highly imaginative schemes using parts of the Apollo hardware were proposed in the years following the start of the moon project. But only one of these fallout space stations ever made it beyond the drawing board—Skylab.

Launch of a Saturn IB.

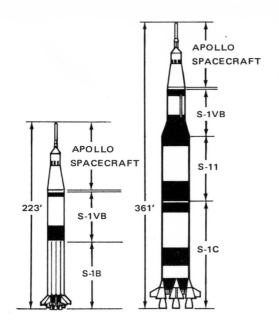

APOLLO
SPACECRAFT

APOLLO
SPACECRAFT

223'

361'

S-1VB

S-1B

S-1VB

S-11

S-1C

The mighty Saturns, having proved their capabilities in the Apollo lunar program, were modified for Skylab. At right, the Saturn V moon rocket. At left, the smaller Saturn IB.

At left, launch of a Saturn V.

Shown under construction, the Payload Shroud. The giant nose cone covered the Apollo Telescope Mount, the Multiple Docking Adapter, and part of the Airlock Module during launch of Skylab.

The Skylab Cluster

3

Engineers at NASA called what was to be America's pioneer space station the Skylab Cluster. It consisted of four major units that remained in space: the Orbital Workshop, the Airlock Module, the Multiple Docking Adapter, and the Apollo Telescope Mount. Temporary additions to the cluster were the Command/Service Modules, which ferried the crews into space and which remained docked at the Multiple Docking Adapter while the men were in residence.

The Orbital Workshop

The heart of Skylab was the Orbital Workshop. This 48.5-foot-long, 21.7-foot-diameter cylinder contained living quarters for the crew, a laboratory for the major portion of the experiments, most of the expendable supplies, and an attitude-control system for proper orientation of Skylab in space.

As has already been pointed out, the design for the Orbital Workshop started with the Saturn IVB rocket stage, and not surprisingly a number of the S-IVB features were retained. In its conversion, the former hydrogen tank contained the two-story living and working area. The smaller oxygen tank—to avoid polluting open space—was turned into an orbiting trash dump for body wastes and other unwanted materials. The immense size of the two-story workshop was little short of staggering when compared with the Mercury, Gemini, and Apollo space vehicles in which for the most part crews were confined to their couches.

A ceiling grid separated the four-room crew quarters from the upper level. Around the curved top of this level were water containers. There was also much experimental apparatus. And there were as well many lockers in which supplies for all three sets of crews were stowed at the time of launch, a necessary measure since few supplies could be sent up in the Command/Service Modules with each new crew.

In space, unbuffered by an atmosphere as we are here on earth,

Skylab was subject to both the intense heat of the sun and to the impact of micrometeoroids. Protection from large meteoroids cannot be provided of course. However, micrometeoroids, which might impact the sides of the space station, could do a considerable amount of damage over a period of time, and Skylab was designed for occupancy over an eight-month period. A shield, made of thin sheets of aluminum and coated with heat-protective paint, was developed to ward off solar rays and to "catch" micrometeoroids. It was held against the sides of the Orbital Workshop during launch. Once the workshop was in orbit, spring-loaded devices were to pop the shield out and hold it about five inches away from the workshop.

This shield was to prove a serious source of trouble. In the first minutes into the launch, air pressure built up under the shield, pushing it away from the side of the workshop where the supersonic airstream ripped it off. As the shield tore away, it broke clamps securing one of the Orbital Workshop's two solar power wings, and the wing was lost nine minutes later. Debris from the torn shield also jammed the second solar power wing, locking it into a closed position. Exposed to the full strength of the sun's rays, deprived of its main power source, the Orbital Workshop lacked the electricity needed to cool it and make it fully functional.

Skylab consumed vast amounts of electricity, to be supplied by the huge solar power wings attached to the outside of the workshop and by the four smaller wings on the Apollo Telescope Mount. The idea was that these two electrical systems—the one getting energy from the workshop's solar power wings and the other from the Apollo Telescope Mount's solar power wings—would deliver power to and draw power from each other. It was a good plan in light of the developments following the launch when power to the workshop was supplied solely by the solar power wings mounted on the Apollo Telescope Mount.

As originally designed, the two large solar power wings on the workshop—stretching 90 feet from the outer edge of one to the outer edge of the other and containing 147,840 energy-producing cells, each 2 by 4 centimeters—were to have supplied the station with more than 10,000 watts of electrical power. Batteries would supply the onboard electrical power when the station was in darkness and would be recharged when the station returned to sunlight and the solar power wings resumed normal function.

Until Conrad and Kerwin took their dangerous space walk and freed the workshop's remaining solar power wing so that it extended and began to supply power to the station, the crippled Skylab had only about one-half normal power, and that came from the four small solar power wings on the Apollo Telescope Mount.

The shift from the Wet to the Dry Workshop concept called for removal of the large engine at the base of the Orbital Workshop since this engine played no part in placing the workshop in orbit. Without this engine, Skylab was not capable of large maneuvers in space. However, small maneuvers were possible in order to maintain the correct position, or attitude. The primary attitude-control system was located on the Apollo Telescope Mount and was augmented by a subsystem on the Orbital Workshop itself. Using the subsystem, maneuvers were performed by six small thrusters powered by cold nitrogen gas stored in bottles at the bottom of the workshop. The thrusters could be operated either by the astronauts themselves or by controllers at Mission Control Center at NASA's Lyndon B. Johnson Space Center in Houston, Texas.

The Apollo Telescope Mount

The 24,656-pound Apollo Telescope Mount was attached to the open trusswork outside the Multiple Docking Adapter and the Airlock Module. From launch to orbit, the ATM sat directly above the Multiple Docking Adapter inside the protective Payload Shroud. Once in orbit, the telescope mount pivoted so that it was at right angles to the Multiple Docking Adapter. Then four wings—the solar array—were unfurled from the ATM, making Skylab look like a gigantic orbiting windmill.

Four years' work went into the ATM solar array. Together, the four wings powered 18 batteries and consisted of 1,200 square feet of solar cells, which generated almost 10,500 watts of electricity. The entire ATM solar array weighed some 4,300 pounds.

The key word in the Apollo Telescope Mount was "telescope." Actually, there were eight telescopes aboard the telescope mount, all focused on the most important member of our solar system, the sun. A solar shield protected the instruments from the sun's harmful radiation; a thermal shield maintained the equipment at operable temperatures.

As with any telescope, those of Skylab had to be pointed accurately and remain locked on an object with infinitesimal accuracy. To keep the ATM from moving and losing the object in view, three huge gyroscopes—each 22 inches in diameter—insured stability. The gyroscopes were the heart of the complex attitude-control system that kept the entire Skylab Cluster properly oriented in the sky. A special pointing system, guided by an error-correcting sun sensor, aimed the telescope mount with an accuracy of 2½ seconds of arc—a feat that might be likened to measuring a distance of 16 feet at 250 miles.

The ATM could be remotely controlled by the crew from a console inside the Multiple Docking Adapter. Television played an important role in the ATM's operation. Five TV cameras located in the telescope mount permitted the men to observe in real time the same views being seen and photographed by the telescopes. Television pictures were displayed on a sophisticated control and display console, and many switches and dials made it possible to point the telescopes to areas of special interest on the sun in order to get the most important pictures. The pictures were sent back to earth in real time to ground-based scientists assisting the crew in pointing and running the telescopes.

The ATM was one of the few pieces of major Skylab hardware not manufactured by an aerospace company. Bits and pieces were built by contractors or at U.S. universities. Assembly of the various elements was then undertaken at the Marshall Space Flight Center in Hunts-

The complicated Apollo Telescope Mount was operated from a control and display console in the Multiple Docking Adapter. Astronauts Alan L. Bean and Jack R. Lousma here operate a realistic mock-up during preflight training.

ville, Alabama, by NASA engineers and technicians. Since a microscopic piece of dust or lint on a telescope or other sensitive component could be disastrous in space, the complete assembly operation was done under ultraclean conditions inside a giant "white room," with everyone wearing white hats, smocks, and "booties."

The actual presence of men in the orbiting observatory was perhaps the most valuable single factor in the astronomical experiments. The astronauts could point the telescopes at the right targets to insure that important events were not missed and valuable film not wasted. They could repair the equipment if the need arose. And they could work in close harmony with astronomers and other experts on the ground to make sure that the instruments were put to best use. The result was the best look at the solar system we have yet had. For example, that part of the sun's ultraviolet and X-ray radiation which does not penetrate the earth's atmosphere and thus is difficult to evaluate from the ground was measured. It will be some time before all the information gathered by Skylab can be coordinated and fully evaluated.

The Multiple Docking Adapter

The Multiple Docking Adapter was a mighty welcome sight to the crews on their journeys from earth to the Skylab Cluster, for it was here the Command/Service Modules hooked onto the space station so that the men could climb aboard for their adventures in space living.

Cylindrical in shape, the MDA had two docking ports, one at the head-on end and the other on the side. According to NASA plans, normally no more than one Command/Service Module would ever be docked with the laboratory at any one time, but the second docking port added a safety factor for an unforeseen emergency. If by some chance the Command/Service Module could not make contact with the prime docking port, it could dock at the side port. Also, if for some reason a crew could not use its Command/Service Module for the return trip home, another one could be launched from earth and could link up with Skylab to rescue the marooned crew.

The MDA did more than function as a pier, however. It was the site of and control center for some of Skylab's major experiments. It was used as a warehouse for space equipment; vaults for storing film were located here, for instance. And it was from the MDA that the Apollo Telescope Mount was controlled—probably the most important job carried on here. Two windows located across from each other permitted the men to watch the Apollo Telescope Mount operate.

Docking targets and running lights located on the outside of the MDA assisted upcoming crews in making their final approach to the workshop. Handrails were located around the outside to assist the crew

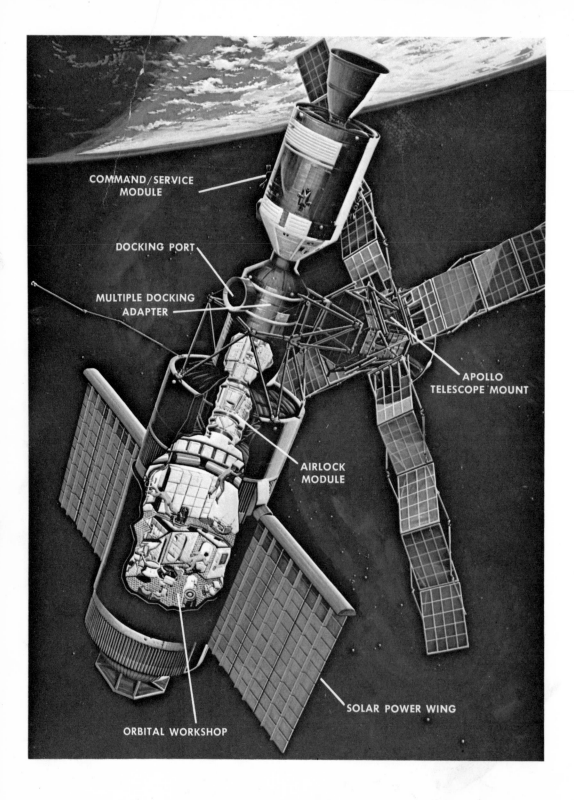

COMMAND/SERVICE
MODULE

DOCKING PORT

MULTIPLE DOCKING
ADAPTER

APOLLO
TELESCOPE MOUNT

AIRLOCK
MODULE

SOLAR POWER WING

ORBITAL WORKSHOP

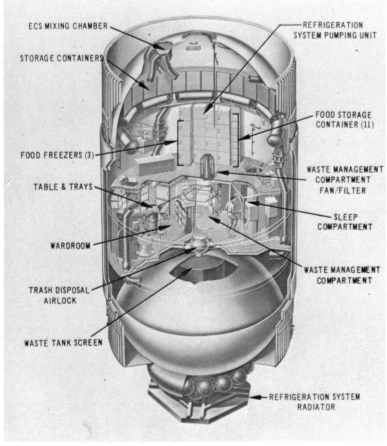

ECS MIXING CHAMBER

STORAGE CONTAINERS

REFRIGERATION
SYSTEM PUMPING UNIT

FOOD STORAGE
CONTAINER (11)

FOOD FREEZERS (3)

TABLE & TRAYS

WARDROOM

TRASH DISPOSAL
AIRLOCK

WASTE TANK SCREEN

WASTE MANAGEMENT
COMPARTMENT
FAN/FILTER

SLEEP
COMPARTMENT

WASTE MANAGEMENT
COMPARTMENT

REFRIGERATION SYSTEM
RADIATOR

Far left, an artist's rendering of a fully operational Skylab. Troubles were not foreseen.

At left, a cutaway view of the Orbital Workshop.

Below, a test version of the Orbital Workshop is loaded aboard the U.S.S. *Point Barrow* for shipment from Seal Beach, California, to Houston, Texas.

WIDE LOAD

when they worked in space. Also mounted outside were radiators which were part of Skylab's cooling system, known in engineering terms as its "environmental control system."

The Airlock Module

Directly below the Multiple Docking Adapter was the Airlock Module. Serving as the passageway between the Multiple Docking Adapter and the Orbital Workshop, the AM was the heart and brain of the Skylab Cluster. In it was housed the equipment that controlled the atmosphere, temperature, and electrical power of most of the Skylab Cluster except for the Apollo Telescope Mount, which had its own control and distribution system. Also located here was equipment for communicating with the ground, intercom equipment for communication between the various parts of the station, a complex electrical system that helped transmit the vast amount of experimental data collected during the mission, and an exit hatch.

Inside the AM was a 5½-foot-diameter by 13-foot-long cylindrical tunnel divided by two hatches into three compartments. The center compartment, large enough to hold two fully suited astronauts with their portable life-support systems, was the exit hatch through which the astronauts stepped into space. They waited here in the chamber until it was depressurized to the zero pressure outside the Skylab Cluster before exiting into space. After their duties were completed, they waited here again while the chamber was repressurized to the level of the rest of the station. The compartments on either side of the exit hatch held such things as spare parts and part of the system that distributed the life-sustaining atmosphere throughout Skylab.

On the AM were a number of large spherical and cylindrical tanks that held the gaseous oxygen and nitrogen used for the station's atmosphere. A Fixed Airlock Shroud covering most of the bottom of the AM hid the tanks from view, making it appear that the module was part of the Orbital Workshop. Actually, it was a completely separate piece of equipment.

The Instrument Unit

Frequently forgotten because it did not function during the actual time men were aboard the space station was the Instrument Unit. It did, however, play an important part during the launch and Skylab's first few hours in orbit. Located between the Airlock Module and the Orbital Workshop, this 21.7-foot-diameter wafer used sophisticated electronics to guide the Saturn V launch vehicle into orbit, to set pressurizing and ventilation machinery to work, and to send futile signals to unfurl the damaged solar power wings, which could not, of course, respond as expected.

The IU was one more part of the Saturn V-Apollo vehicle that had already proved itself on many trips to the moon, steering the Saturn V into earth orbit and directing its S-IV B third stage to push the Apollo spacecraft onward in its voyage to the moon.

The Payload Shroud

The giant Payload Shroud, or nose cone, covered the Apollo Telescope Mount, the Multiple Docking Adapter, and part of the Airlock Module during the launch of Skylab into space. At 66 feet in length, with a 21.7-foot diameter, this was the largest nose cone ever used in the U.S. space program. Constructed of four identical pieces, the shroud separated from the Skylab Cluster about midway into the first orbit. The separation was accomplished by explosives lining the seams between the four pieces. When the explosives ignited, the four panels fell away, rather like the peeling of a banana, without touching the cluster and inflicting harmful damage.

Not only did the PS allow Skylab to slice through the dense atmosphere; it also provided protection from the elements before and during launch. Several access doors in the shroud permitted technicians to work on Skylab while launch preparations moved ahead.

The Command/Service Modules

Used for shuttling crews to and from the space station, the Command/Service Modules were nearly identical with those used in the lunar program. In fact, no new CSMs were built for the Skylab program. Those used were left over from the Apollo program but were somewhat modified for this new application. Modifications were necessary because of the extended length of the Skylab mission, because the vehicles had to rendezvous and dock with Skylab, and finally because they had to return a payload of unprecedented weight to earth.

The modules had to be prepared to remain in space almost 60 days in the Skylab program as opposed to the up-to-14-day stays of the Apollo missions. While docked with the space station, the CSM was in a powered-down condition most of the time. Longer-life batteries had to be installed and valves in the rocket engine modified so that the CSM could be started for the trip home after almost 60 days.

In the Skylab role, the rocket engine did not need as much propellant as it did when it had to perform maneuvers to get into and out of lunar orbit. Consequently, two propellant tanks and a helium pressure bottle were removed from the Service Module.

The first ground test version of an Apollo Telescope Mount, here shown during assembly at the Marshall Space Flight Center in Huntsville, Alabama.

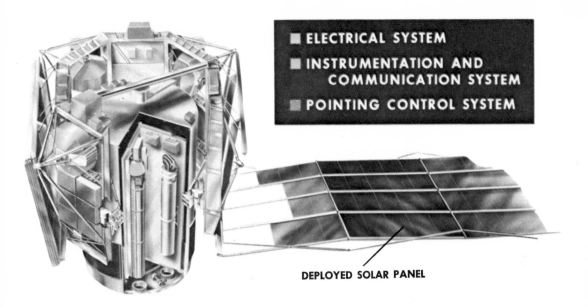

■ ELECTRICAL SYSTEM

■ INSTRUMENTATION AND COMMUNICATION SYSTEM

■ POINTING CONTROL SYSTEM

DEPLOYED SOLAR PANEL

A cutaway view of one of the canisters used in the Apollo Telescope Mount.

Command/Service Modules used to ferry astronauts to and from Skylab were modified versions of those used in the Apollo lunar program.

Further plans had been made for the CSMs, with the hope that such plans would never need to be executed. These involved a Skylab rescue operation.

The CSM parked at the docking port was in a semiquiescent state, but instant readiness was assured. Heaters maintained vital parts at proper operating temperatures, and the crew regularly monitored the equipment. In case of an emergency, say a fire or an explosion, the men could grab portable oxygen bottles, scramble into their CSM "lifeboat," and set out for home.

If for some reason the CSM could not be used, the rescue plan called for a Saturn I B to be rapidly dispatched to its launch pad, stowage lockers stripped out of the Command Module, and two extra couches installed. Two men could then take the craft up to the space station and dock at the alternate port, the three marooned crewmen could clamber aboard, and the five men could return to earth. The Saturn I B used for such a rescue mission would be the one normally scheduled for the next crew-replacement mission and thus would be near the end of its assembly and check-out. Rescue plans for the last crew involved use of the Skylab backup spacecraft. It had been

The Airlock Module through which the astronauts passed on entering or leaving the Orbital Workshop. Here the men waited after docking until it was certain the workshop was in working order. And here space-suited crewmen underwent depressurization and repressurization before and after space walks.

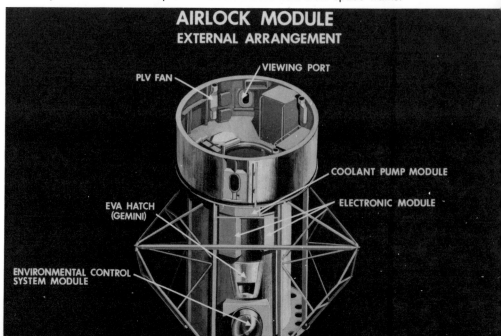

AIRLOCK MODULE
EXTERNAL ARRANGEMENT

PLV FAN

VIEWING PORT

COOLANT PUMP MODULE

EVA HATCH
(GEMINI)

ELECTRONIC MODULE

ENVIRONMENTAL CONTROL
SYSTEM MODULE

estimated that such a craft could be readied for launch in about eight weeks.

When troubles involving a serious fuel leak in the CSM developed on August 2, 1973, only six days into the second mission, the rescue plan was put into operation. It was expected that the rescue craft could have been ready for launch about two weeks before the scheduled return to earth of the second crew. Fortunately it was not neeessary to activate the rescue plan.

The Saturns

The giant Skylab Cluster was placed in orbit by the powerful Saturn V rocket, a two-stage rocket—the first stage an S-IC, the second an S-II. The crews were launched by modified two-stage Saturn IB rockets— the first stage an S-IB, the second stage an S-IVB.

The entire Saturn V-Skylab combination towered some 334 feet high, only about 30 feet less than the Saturn V-Apollo combination, and weighed some 6,222,000 pounds. The five first-stage engines produced as much power as 85 Hoover Dams in a given moment, and each of the powerful pumps providing propellant to the engines could have emptied a 20,000-gallon swimming pool in less than a minute. In orbit, the Skylab Cluster weighed about 200,000 pounds.

The Skylab launch was the first time the Saturn V had used only two stages; all previous Apollo launches used all three. And its payload capability was over 214,000 pounds from earth into the Skylab orbit.

It had been a number of years since a Saturn was built. All the Saturns eventually used in the Skylab program had been kept in storage, and the length of storage time was a subject of concern to NASA officials, for after all there was no way of knowing with absolute certainty how well the giant boosters had withstood the dormant years.

The Saturns had been kept in firing condition, however; periodically, critical parts, such as seals and gaskets, had been checked to make sure the vehicles were in tip-top condition. In 1971 a Saturn IB rocket had been removed from storage after almost nine years in hibernation and performed as well as it did when brand new. The Saturn IB used for the first manned Skylab launch was built in 1966 and had been in a state of inactivity for three years before undergoing modification for the Skylab program. With the special inspection and preservation procedures developed during this period, NASA now feels that the Saturns can be stored for many years, taken out, and fired successfully.

The equipment described here took thousands of man-years to develop, build, and test. Skylab was now ready for action. It was only necessary to add the one most important ingredient of all—*man*.

The "Skylab 500." Poised for a rapid start in their race around the dome of the Orbital Workshop are astronauts Conrad, Kerwin, and Weitz. Via TV, they demonstrated great ease of motion in the weightless conditions of space.

Living in Space

$$4$$

No longer were U.S. astronauts confined to quarters about as roomy as an aircraft cockpit. Space travel had come of age, and men—living and working for several months in isolation from all other human beings—had in Skylab a space home that was in its way as convenient as an efficiency apartment. There was room both to move—or should we say bound—about and a degree of privacy for each man.

Living and Working Quarters

The crew quarters, containing both living and working areas, were spacious enough to set up a handball court. Players would have a hard time moving around, though, because of the unusual grid floor. The triangular pattern of the grid had a very special purpose, however. The astronauts wore boots that, with a slight twist, locked into the floor, holding steady as the men performed their duties.

The "first floor" of the workshop, something less than 400 square feet of living area, was divided into four compartments: the wardroom, the experiment compartment, the sleep compartment, and the waste management compartment. The compartments were separated by solid partitions.

The sleep compartment had three broom-closet-sized bedrooms, separated by hard walls and fabric doors. Each had a "bed," or sleep restraint, a sleeping-bag arrangement that fastened to the ceiling and floor grids to prevent the sleeper from floating around. The sleep restraints were placed in what we would consider a vertical position since there was no gravity in the Orbital Workshop, and a good deal of space was thus conserved. Each sleep compartment also had an intercom, a light, and six small lockers for personal items, and there were light-baffling devices in the ceiling to darken the cubicle if the astronaut wished.

Located on one wall of the waste management compartment was a zero-gravity "toilet" and a hand washer. Waste processors and storage cabinets for supplies lined the other walls. The compartment was separately sealed from the rest of the workshop with walls and doors to retain odors and particles that might cause problems in the weightless environment.

One of the most interesting areas of the Orbital Workshop was the wardroom, where meals were cooked, where the men might spend their free time, and where the inevitable bull sessions took place. Occupying the center of the compartment was a mess table surrounded by zero-gravity "chairs"—actually foot and thigh restraints that held the men in a semiseated position while they ate. Each man's tray had eight food niches, four for large containers and four for small ones. Three of the larger niches were heated and had timers to control the length of cooking time of food in the trays. In the center of the table were hot-cold water guns for reconstituting dry food, such as powdered milk and freeze-dried coffee. Individual drinking dispensers, thought necessary to reduce the chance of spreading bacteria, were mounted at the sides of the table. They were fitted with color-coded mouthpieces—one color for each crewman—and dispensed chilled drinking water.

A really special feature of the wardroom was a doubled-paned window, 18 inches in diameter. Heated to prevent fogging and always facing the earth, it was "just for looking." It took a great amount of persuasion on the astronauts' part to get the window installed.

By far the largest room in the crew quarters, the experimental area, containing about 180 square feet, had trash disposal facilities, much equipment for experiments to be carried out aboard Skylab, and such large pieces of experimental equipment as the lower-body negative-pressure device and the bicycle ergometer. Here also were stored tool kits and spare parts for making repairs.

Running through the workshop's center was a collapsible and movable fireman's pole for moving between the "upper" and "lower" levels. The men could not slide down the pole, of course, since there is no downward pull in space. But it was an aid in maneuvering between the levels. Incidentally, the words "upper" and "lower" for the two levels of the workshop are earth-oriented terms. Actually there is no "up" or "down" in space. For descriptive convenience, though, we will stick to this terminology.

The upper level was by far the larger portion of the Orbital Workshop. Here the men could float around to their hearts' content. However, that was not the best way to move if there was work to do, and so here as well as in other parts of Skylab, handholds and handrails were placed at strategic locations. They were painted blue to distinguish them from pipes and conduits. Below the entry hatch, located in the dome, was a stowage ring where water tanks and lockers were

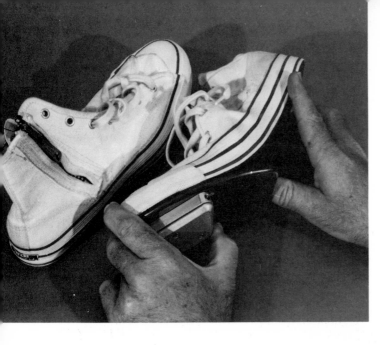

The wedges on the soles of these space shoes were designed to interlock with the grid floor of Skylab, giving the men the stability necessary for certain jobs. However, the shoes were somewhat less effective than planned, and the crewmen reported some difficulties with them.

located. Also in the upper level were food lockers, freezers, and more experimental materials.

Skylab was both heated and air-conditioned. A thermal control and ventilation system gave the astronauts a temperature range of between 60° and 90° F. The men breathed a combination of 24% to 28% nitrogen and 72% oxygen, referred to as a two-gas system. (Earth's atmosphere, by comparison, contains roughly 21% oxygen and 79% nitrogen.) Skylab was the first U.S. manned craft with such a system.

Light fixtures, mostly located in the ceilings, were generously scattered throughout the workshop and could be individually controlled. Portable lights were also available as needed, and in addition, special floodlights could be used when the astronauts worked outside in space.

Fire extinguishers were also placed in critical locations throughout the workshop. Designers, concerned about the crew's safety, built into Skylab a sensitive fire-detection system, which could quickly alert the men to overheating or flame in any part of the space station.

Personal Gear, Tools, Equipment, Supplies

Packing for this trip would have made even the most experienced traveler shudder. Everything to sustain three three-man crews for 140 or more days had to be stowed in Skylab for the initial launch because only a limited amount of equipment would be sent up with the crews. It took great planning, then, to insure that everything the men needed would be in the space station when wanted and that they would be able to find each item in the particular cranny in which it had been tucked away. An elaborate numbering system identified the placement

The bicycle ergometer was used by the Skylab astronauts to measure their ability to exercise in the weightlessness of space. After almost a month at zero gravity, astronauts Kerwin and Weitz, their cardiovascular systems weakened, were unable to perform at preflight levels.

Effects of zero gravity on the circulatory system were studied with the lower-body negative-pressure device. Although abnormalities were reported by several crewmen during the course of the Skylab mission, the difficulties were temporary and disappeared when the men returned to earth.

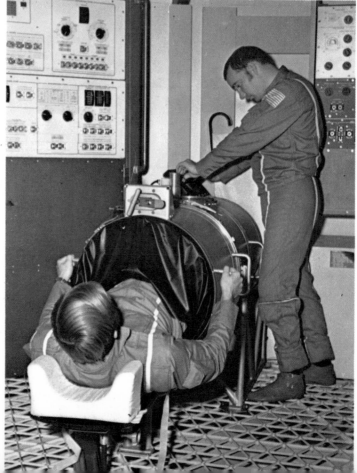

A back-mounted rocket pack was tested during the Skylab mission. Future space stations may be placed in orbit in pieces to be assembled there by men wearing automatically stabilized maneuvering units not unlike the one shown here.

Each crewman had his own sleep compartment, fitted with personal storage space and a sleep restraint. Although astronauts generally slept comfortably and in many positions, Dr. Kerwin said, "If you ever want people on other than a simultaneous sleep cycle, you must provide them with soundproof sleeping accommodations, which is the exact opposite of what we have right now."

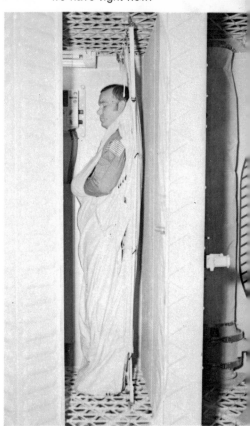

of all materials. Following are some of the more than 20,000 items that were packed into every usable corner of the Orbital Workshop.

Six cylindrical tanks of oxygen weighing some 4,930 pounds were mounted within the Fixed Airlock Shroud, and six spherical tanks of nitrogen weighing 1,320 pounds were mounted on the external Airlock Module trusses.

Ten containers holding 6,000 pounds of potable water were mounted on the stowage ring in the upper level of the workshop. Water from these containers was fed into the workshop. Food, about 2,100 pounds of it, was stored in 5 food freezers and 11 food lockers in the upper level and in the wardroom.

Clothing was packed into 15 clothing modules located in lockers in the wardroom. Some of the more than 700 items included 3 jackets, 53 trousers, 58 shirts, 15 pairs of boots, 15 pairs of gloves, 4 union suits, 47 half union suits, 152 shorts, 199 T-shirts, and 128 pairs of socks. The gold-colored shirts, jackets, and trousers, tailored to the astronauts' dimensions, were made of fire-resistant fabric. Each jacket had an American flag on the upper portion of the left sleeve, the NASA emblem on the upper right front section, and the crew emblem and astronaut's name tag on the upper left front section. The supply of clothing was sufficient to permit the men to change trousers once a week and shirts, underwear, and socks every other day.

Doctors tried to prepare for every emergency, and so a large supply of medical material was placed aboard. There were instruments—scissors, forceps, hemostats, and scalpels—for performing minor surgery, such as extracting small foreign objects from the skin or for closing small cuts and punctures. Also included were 20 different kinds of bandages and dressings and a 20-piece tooth-extraction kit for use in the event of a space toothache.

Some 190 separate packages of pills, ointments, and other medicines were also loaded prior to launch. Unfortunately, drugs were among the items seriously affected by the intense heat inside the Orbital Workshop during the first few days of the Skylab mission, and therefore a fresh supply of many of the drugs was carried into orbit aboard Conrad, Weitz, and Kerwin's Command/Service Module.

Additional miscellaneous gear included 55 bars of soap, 210 pounds of towels and wipes, 54 pounds of tissues, 1,800 urine and fecal bags, 700 pounds of spare parts, tweezers, twine, tape, wire, cameras, film magazines, pens, pencils, rolls of teleprinter paper, 88 pounds of off-duty equipment, a micrometeoroid repair kit—and one vacuum cleaner.

More than 100 hand tools were packed into two toolboxes. Besides the ordinary assortment of wrenches and pliers, there were specialized tools. For working in inaccessible places, there was a retrieval mirror, a hook, and a spring-loaded gadget with mechanical fingers. To enable the crew to make in-flight repairs and to replace parts, there were other tools and miscellaneous pieces of gear such as light bulbs, filters, and batteries.

When the extent of the crippled space station's damages had been assessed, engineers developed other and unique gadgets for replacing the damaged micrometeoroid shield and repairing the solar power wing. One such tool was a metal cutter that was attached to a 25-foot-long pole. It was with this improvised tool that astronauts Conrad and Kerwin cut a defiant piece of metal and thus freed the workshop's one remaining solar power wing during the most daring space repair job in space history.

Food, clothing, and supplies could not be figured down to the last item, of course, for there was no way to predict what the need for certain items would be. Extras, then, were carried aboard, with care taken not to overload the space station. Weight was not the critical factor it had been with other space launches, but it was still a point to be taken into consideration. In all, equipment and supplies totaled more than six tons. Since there is no weight in space, those six tons, once in orbit, weighed nothing.

Eating, Sleeping, and Living Aboard Skylab

Even considering the difficulties the first crew had to contend with, the daily routine aboard Skylab was more relaxed than it was on the Apollo flights. The astronauts lived in surroundings not unlike those they might find on earth. A full eight hours' sleep was scheduled for each night. The crew took about three hours a day for meals and ate them together, giving them a chance to discuss the problems and happenings of the flight. NASA had even scheduled days off, about one a week.

For the first four nights after Conrad, Weitz, and Kerwin joined the problem-ridden Skylab, they returned to the Command/Service Module or the connecting tunnel to sleep and rest. On Tuesday, May 29, 1973, the men actually slept in the space station, and full-time occupancy of the crew quarters had begun. After that, totally aside from the spectacular circumstances in which they were living, all the crews' daily routine was pretty much like one on earth.

After rising at 6:00 A.M. Houston time, each trio had a leisurely breakfast and began their workday. In addition to the technical work, they shared housekeeping tasks, fixing meals, and keeping the station neat. After the evening meal, they discussed the activities planned for the following day and then relaxed with taped music or books. Lights were shut off at 10:00 P.M. Houston time, and the men climbed into their sacks for the night.

Lobster, asparagus, prime rib, salmon, and veal . . . . Does that sound like the menu of an expensive restaurant? It was only a part of the selection of foods available to the astronauts.

Meals on Skylab were more appetizing than those of previous space-flights primarily because of advancements that allowed frozen and canned foods to be added to the Skylab menu. Canned foods were not, however, like those on supermarket shelves. Earth-type cans are packed at 15 pounds per square inch of pressure, and in Skylab these would literally have exploded under the 5 pounds per square inch of cabin pressure. Thus, specially packed cans were stowed away aboard the workshop before launch.

More than 70 different food items were packed in Skylab's freezers and food chests. All of it was taste-tested prior to flight by the crew members so that the food would be familiar and pleasing to the men when they ate it in orbit. Nutrition, color, aroma, texture, and taste were the criteria used by the food planners.

A typical day's menu might begin with Corn Flakes or Rice Crispies served with dried milk, dried fruit, and cocoa or instant coffee. For lunch there might be a cheese sandwich made with a cheese spread and defrosted bread, meat cooked in chili sauce, and coffee, tea, or milk. For dinner there might be turkey with gravy, whipped potatoes, peaches in their natural juices, cookies, and a beverage. Each man's diet consisted of about 2,500 calories per day, but there was extra food, up to 300 calories per day, in case hunger pangs set in and a midnight snack was needed. The 2,500 calories was slightly less than the 3,000 recommended for men their age, so there would be no worry about any of the astronauts outgrowing their space suits.

Each day one man was designated cook of the day, and it was his job to choose the menu, take the food from the freezers and lockers, and place it in the wells in each astronaut's tray. He set the timers on the food warmers and covered the trays with their removable lids, and the foods heated and/or thawed while other duties were attended to. After each meal the food trays were emptied and refilled for the next meal.

The menu was an improvement over those of previous flights, but eating habits were still strange in zero-gravity conditions. Plastic covers on containers kept food from floating away, and magnetic knife and fork holders anchored eating utensils in place. But liquids and loose and crumbly foods were still difficult to handle. A liquid-filled cup moved too fast would still result in an empty cup with the liquid suspended in midair. Peas and beans did not stay on a fork if the fork was interrupted in its movement to the mouth; for once the fork stopped, the vegetables kept moving right off the fork and on across the room. The problems were somewhat solved by liquids being served in expandable plastic bottles, and the astronauts drank almost like babies taking their bottles. To keep food on their forks, the men learned to lift the food to their mouths in one continuous motion. In addition, to help in the handling of loose foods, some came prepared in a sticky sauce or syrup that held the parts together.

When it was time to bed down, or maybe "bed up" is the more correct term, each crewman went to his own compartment for privacy and isolation from the light and noise in the rest of the station. His sleep restraint allowed him to sleep in just about any position that was comfortable, including curled up.

Commander Charles Conrad is shown during preflight training dropping a plastic waste bag through the trash-disposal airlock in the floor of the crew compartment. In the unpressurized tank, bags inflated like balloons.

On relatively short spaceflights, body odor was one thing that could, although perhaps not pleasantly, be lived with. But on longer missions, a clean body became a necessity both for good health and for comfort.

For the daily washing of hands and face, there was a hand-washing device in Skylab's waste management compartment. It was an 18-inch-diameter sphere with armholes lined with rubber flaps. To wash up, the crewman put his hands through the armholes. Water was dispensed into a washcloth, and a squeezer wrung out the excess. Waste water was collected in a bag for later disposal. Magnetized soap dishes held bars of soap, each with a metal bar inserted in its center.

The soap was carefully chosen. Doctors did not want to use anything that might disturb the skin's natural bacteria, since this might interfere with the important medical studies. Further, it was important that the soap not cause a rash or any other skin irritation and that it be a thorough cleanser. And finally, because water was at a premium, the soapsuds had to be easily removed with a very small amount of water.

Each man had his own color-coded hygiene kit containing shaving and dental equipment, soap, emollient, swabs, lotion, a hairbrush, hair cream, nail clippers, deodorant, expectorant collectors, and dental floss. Each astronaut had a daily allotment of two washcloths, each hemmed in red, white, or blue so that the man could identify his own. Towels were similarly marked.

Showering aboard Skylab was an interesting experience, especially since each man was allotted only three quarts of water for a shower once a week. The preferred technique was the wet-soap-rinse routine. The crewman undressed, raised a circular enclosure, and attached it to the ceiling gridwork. A pushbutton-controlled shower nozzle with a flexible hose attached to a portable water bottle permitted him to wash all parts of his body. When he was finished, he vacuumed himself dry; a flexible hose with a vacuum attachment drew the used water into a disposable bag, which was then deposited in the waste tank.

Disposing of trash and body wastes for nine men during a 143-day period presented something of a sanitation engineering problem. To further complicate matters, much of the body wastes had to be saved, stored, and shipped back to earth as part of Skylab's medical experiment.

The so-called collector module, mounted on one wall of the waste management compartment, was the space equivalent of an earth toilet. Used while the astronaut was in a seated position, facing the compartment floor, the zero-gravity "toilet" allowed defecation and urination at the same time. A lap belt and two handholds kept the user from floating away at a time when he would least want to. A suction blower located behind the wall of the compartment drew waste matter into a plastic bag.

To insure cleanliness of the living area and the good health of the crew, any item considered biologically active—clothing, towels, washcloths, sleep restraints, food cans, and so on—had to be disposed of as quickly as possible. Two types of waste bags were available for trash collection. When they were filled, they were dropped into the below-floor waste tank through the trash-disposal airlock in the floor of the crew compartment.

Off-Hours in Space

With the length of time each crew would be aboard Skylab, recreation for the men was a potential problem to be considered. Boredom probably would not be a difficulty, for the days would be packed with experiments to run, meals to be prepared and eaten, and housekeeping duties to be tended to. The very uniqueness of the situation would itself be a boredom preventative. However, everyone needs a break in the daily routine now and then, and the flight plan took this into account.

A considerable amount of taped music went up with Skylab—some four-dozen cassettes, which could be played either through the speaker system or through individual headsets. Each astronaut had his own personal music library.

Also stowed aboard was a small library of paperbacks, chosen by the men themselves, and some books of a general nature like a world almanac and a book of world records to settle arguments.

Four decks of cards, made of fire-resistant paper, were included so the men could play a few hands of poker or gin rummy. Other gear included pens and pencils for making personal notes in diaries, a set of binoculars, and two microphones for the crews' use in recording their comments on tape.

Mounted in front of the book section was a Velcro-pile-covered dart board. The darts, blue and gold, had heads covered with Velcro hook. Three handballs of varying size, Exer-Gyms, and hand exercisers were also on board to help these physical-fitness enthusiasts keep their muscles hard.

For really strenuous entertainment, the men could go "upstairs" to "run" around the water tanks or to perform zero-gravity acrobatics to the music from the movie *2001—Space Odyssey* as the first crew did for the amusement of the folks back home.

Two floors of living and working area, with the space equivalents of kitchens, bedrooms, and bathrooms. A two-gas atmosphere. Baths and changes of clothing. Lobster and prime rib. Music and books and dart games. Space travel has progressed far from its first days of crude experimentation just a short decade ago.

During a 1½-hour space walk on June 19, 1973, the so-called handyman astronauts of SL-2 once again proved their ability to get the job done. While Conrad hammered a battery back into operation and retrieved exposed film from the solar telescopes, Weitz radioed a description of the event. This was the fourth extravehicular activity of the first mission.

The Skylab Experiments

5

Skylab's reason for being? Its basic purpose? To provide a space platform for scientific experiments, some of which would give us information about the sun and stars undistorted by the earth's atmosphere, some of which would provide new information about the earth, some of which would tell us more about man and just how he reacts to a weightless environment for extended periods of time, and some of which would suggest ways in which a zero-gravity environment might be used by man. Although it would take years to fully evaluate the results of the experiments, it was certain such studies would tell us more about the earth, man, and space than we had ever known.

Fifty-four experimental packages, containing more than 270 experiments, were a part of the Skylab flight plan. Some experiments were performed by all three crews—for example, blood sampling, tests using the lower-body negative-pressure device, and certain camera studies. Others were done only on specific flights: sleep monitoring on manned flights 1 and 2, the effects of zero gravity on single human cells on flight 1, possible disturbances of the circadian rhythms of pocket mice on flight 2, and crew/vehicle disturbance on flight 3. Many of the experiments were highly complicated, and much of the astronauts' preflight training involved learning to operate and monitor the equipment. The task presented a great technical challenge even to the highly educated astronauts.

Earth Resources Experiments

The six instruments in this package were designed to examine the earth. With cameras, sensors, and scanners which operated simultaneously or independently, astronauts and scientists alike gained information useful in surveying the earth's environment and resources on a global scale.

One experiment consisted of six precisely aligned cameras, each of which recorded data from the same area of the earth's surface but each at a different wavelength. This provided more information than could be captured by ordinary photography. For example, ordinary photographic equipment could not show the difference between diseased and healthy crops, but at infrared wavelengths the differences were easily seen. The six-camera combination provided square surface coverage of approximately 88 nautical miles. When used together, as they ultimately will be, these photos will map the earth to a degree of accuracy never before known. In addition to the six-camera system, a single-lens camera capable of providing square surface coverage of about 59 nautical miles provided color pictures of large sections of the earth's surface.

Highly technical sensors and scanners also peered down at the earth, recording data on magnetic tape. Microwave sensors that could "see" through heavy cloud covers provided additional information when Skylab passed over clouded areas.

From all this it was expected that information would be gathered not only on vegetation, but on mineral deposits, water supplies, seasonal variations in vegetation, snow cover, flooding, roughness and precise temperatures of the oceans in the world's remotest places, population distribution, and land usage.

Most of the earth resources experiments required two astronauts to operate the equipment.

Life Sciences Experiments

Could man live for months or even years without feeling the reassuring pull of gravity on his body? And if so, what effect would weightlessness have on the millions of cells and organs that constitute his body? Would his body change so that later he would experience temporary or even permanent complications from space travel? The many medical experiments were designed to find answers to these and related questions.

In flight, samples of body wastes and blood were taken, stored in sealed containers, and returned to earth with the men in their Command/Service Modules. The samples were then analyzed to detect any changes that might have taken place during flight. Medical technicians also hoped to find out if possible changes in the men's hormonal or chemical makeup had occurred and whether their immunity to disease had been reduced.

In an experiment designed to test nutritional and musculoskeletal functions, the astronauts' food intake was exactly measured and weighed. Body eliminations were then precisely measured, and by comparing input to output, doctors found out how the men gained or lost weight in zero gravity. Still another experiment was designed to

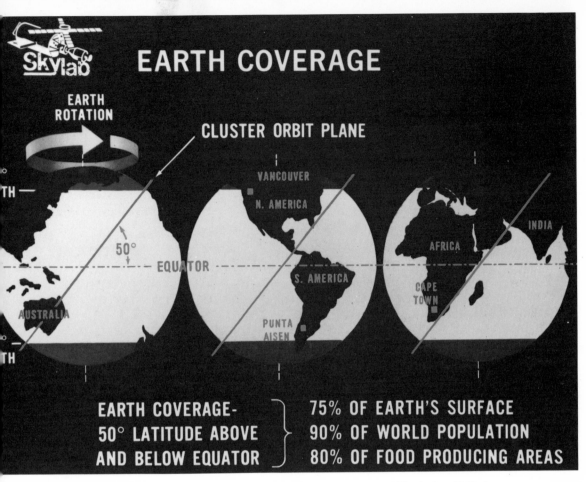

EARTH COVERAGE

Skylab

EARTH ROTATION

CLUSTER ORBIT PLANE

VANCOUVER
N. AMERICA
INDIA
AFRICA
50°
EQUATOR
S. AMERICA
CAPE TOWN
AUSTRALIA
PUNTA AISEN

EARTH COVERAGE-
50° LATITUDE ABOVE
AND BELOW EQUATOR

} 75% OF EARTH'S SURFACE
90% OF WORLD POPULATION
80% OF FOOD PRODUCING AREAS

Orbiting the earth every 93 minutes, Skylab passed over all of the United States and much of the world. The space station's earth resources experiments viewed and recorded information about the earth over a swath width that ranged from one to 88 nautical miles.

show the effects of zero gravity on human cells. The astronauts took time-lapse pictures of living human cells. These tissue cultures were then brought back to earth for later medical analysis.

The men were given complete physicals, including X rays, before and after their flights. Postflight X rays then determined whether or not there had been a breakdown, or demineralization, of the men's bones, and if so, to what degree demineralization occurred. The areas particularly studied were the heel bone and the right forearm.

In the lower-body negative-pressure experiment, a crewman entered a device that enclosed the lower half of his body. This device, which collected data on blood pressure, heart rate, body temperature, leg-volume changes, and other physical conditions, provided information on heart activity during the flight and gave an indication of the amount of physical difficulty the astronaut could expect when he returned to earth.

In another experiment, an astronaut worked out on the bicycle ergometer, testing his ability to work in the weightlessness of space. And in still another experiment, a crewman sat or lay in a revolving litter chair, eyes blindfolded, while the chair was spun to create an artificial gravity. While the chair spun, the crewman recorded his sensations on a tape recorder and also performed simple tasks to determine the possible presence of disorientation problems.

Sleep patterns were analyzed, too. Wired up for bed, the crewman wore a helmet that permitted brain waves and eye movements to be monitored. The results were compared with preflight and postflight monitorings to determine the effects of zero gravity on sleep.

Study of spaceflight was to have extended beyond the men to a group of passengers. Sent up with the second crew was a group of mice for what was known as the circadian rhythm-pocket mice experiment. The purpose of the experiment was to determine whether the 24-hour biological rhythm (the circadian rhythm) of a mammal's system varied under spaceflight conditions. The plan called for a 28-day collection of data on body temperature, heartbeat, and activity level. Located in the Service Module, the package containing the experiment was completely automatic, and the data was to have been automatically returned to earth. Other guests aboard the second Service Module were a number of vinegar gnats, part of another completely automatic experiment. The purpose here was to see what effect changes of temperature in space had on the gnats' life cycle. Disappointingly, neither of these experiments was to be concluded.

So in this first space station, every motion and action of the astronauts and their caged guests were monitored and studied. Skylab was the first American space mission with the acquisition of life sciences data as one of its foremost goals. Doctors and bioscientists made the most of this opportunity.

Engineering and Technology Experiments

The whole time from lift-off to touchdown was in itself an experiment —with some unexpected curves thrown in for good measure, for nobody could have predicted the misfortunes that were to plague Skylab during the entire flight and the means that would be devised to put it into working order. Nowhere in all those preflight plans was there an order for a space walk to pry loose a jammed solar power wing, or to set up an umbrellalike covering to replace the damaged micrometeoroid shield, or to later mount a replacement for that shield, or to start a battery functioning by hitting it with a hammer, or to warm up a nearly frozen cooling unit by wrapping it in a heated space jacket. And yet these things happened and were successful.

Observations in general included data on everything each crew used in daily life, from the instrumentation to the kitchen facilities. Movies were taken while the men worked all the gadgets, and there were frequent talk sessions with the ground to iron out problems.

On future space stations, extravehicular activities may be greatly increased. In fact, future space stations may be placed into orbit in pieces and assembled there by the astronauts. With this future activity in mind, the men tested the automatically stabilized maneuvering unit, a back-mounted rocket pack. The rocket pack's 14 small thrusters, fed with high-pressure nitrogen gas, enabled the astronauts to move about inside Skylab with some ease. In addition to the rocket pack, they also experimented with a small hand-held maneuvering unit, which plugged into the rocket pack for its propellant.

Another interesting piece of equipment was a foot-controlled maneuvering unit. When working outside a space station, an astronaut often must be in a position slightly back from the spacecraft. To free his hands for work, a foot-operated power unit was tested. It was a device that looked a lot like a saddle. The astronaut straddled it and operated little foot levers much as he would the accelerator on a car. He could even turn the unit around without touching it with his hands.

Extravehicular activity was scheduled for all the manned flights. It was planned that two fully suited crewmen would work outside Skylab while the third crewman, located forward of the Airlock Module, monitored their activities. Three hours from leaving the spaceship to reentering it was considered the maximum. However, the flight plan was slightly altered to permit Charles Conrad and Joseph Kerwin to extend their space walk on June 7, 1973, to 3 hours and 25 minutes, a new record. The flight plan was vastly altered and that record smashed when Owen Garriott and Jack Lousma, of the second crew, remained "outdoors" for a total of 6 hours and 31 minutes. William Pogue and Edward Gibson of the last crew extended this record by over six minutes.

Since many of the experiments required extremely high pointing accuracy on the part of the station, it was necessary to determine early in the mission how the movement of the astronauts inside the space station affected its stability. Using a device that measured the motion of the crewmen, the effects of the motion were monitored to determine whether changes had occurred in Skylab's attitude.

The astronauts were also asked to see how well they could function as navigators. Using hand-held instruments that measured the angles between various stars and between stars and the lunar surface, they made space-navigation measurements through a window.

The check-out of all the parts of Skylab and the development of techniques for using its equipment provided much knowledge that will be put to use in space stations and space voyages in the future.

Manufacturing Experiments

Products manufactured on earth are inevitably influenced by the effects of gravity. It was suspected that in a weightless environment, in which there is no effect of the pull of earth's gravity on matter, familiar materials might react in new ways and even that entirely new products, with unique and superior qualities, might be developed. Crystals might form differently. Magnetic properties might be altered. Possibly new alloys might be produced.

The manufacturing experiments were carried out in a 16-inch-diameter sphere vented to the deep vacuum of space. The work chamber contained an electron beam subsystem, and in the chamber wall

Water behaves unpredictably in zero gravity, as Dr. Kerwin demonstrates.

were several small electric furnaces, one of which could achieve temperatures of 1,832° F. and then cool rapidly. Welding and casting of metals were done, and molten flow, freezing patterns, and crystal growth were observed. It was speculated that in the space environment perfect crystals might form, which would have potential use in the semiconductors needed for precision electronics, and that perfect ball bearings could be manufactured.

Fires in space vehicles have always been a worry, and information was needed about better ways to prevent and control them. Thus, flammability tests were conducted as part of the manufacturing program. Fuel samples were ignited in the closed work chamber, and through viewports the crew watched what happened, took pictures, and tried to put out the flames in different ways.

Skylab offered the first real opportunity to investigate the advantages of manufacturing without gravity. The experiments carried out in the manufacturing series may someday lead to space factories in which the weightless characteristics of space will be employed to produce extremely pure and ultrastrong materials. And the experiments may also contribute to the handling of materials and the construction of stations in space.

Solar Physics and Astrophysics Experiments

The sun dominates our solar system, helping to control our climate and representing a tremendous source of energy that may someday be harnessed, helping to prevent power shortages on earth. But before solar energy can be put to use, or its effect on the weather controlled, much more knowledge of solar radiation is required. Experiments conducted from the Apollo Telescope Mount provided basic information previously unavailable to earth-bound astronomers hampered by earth's atmosphere in obtaining clear photographs of solar displays.

No astronomical instrument on earth or in space is perfectly rigid. Yet the nine solar experiments were planned so that the instruments were aligned. Each instrument was directed toward the same point on the sun's surface in such a manner that it remained stable to within 1/700 of a degree for a 15-minute period, thus minimizing the blurring of photographic images.

Two telescopes sensitive to the light emitted by the hydrogen near the sun's surface measured the intensity of the sun's flares. Another instrument measured the intensity of the sun's corona, which extends vast distances into space. And in another experiment, the sun's X-ray activities were photographed, providing data to be used in determining corona temperatures.

Of the nine astrophysics experiments, three studied the outer atmosphere of the earth and interplanetary space while six studied objects external to our solar system. One interesting study was the Gegenschein/zodiacal light experiment, which investigated two phenomena of interplanetary space. Gegenschein, a faint light opposite the sun, can be viewed only when there is no moonlight. Zodiacal light can be observed in the west after twilight and in the east before dawn. Scientists believe these lights are caused by sunlight reflecting from interplanetary material. The equipment aboard Skylab enabled the astronauts to measure the brightness of these lights.

Another astrophysics experiment investigated the minute particles, micrometeoroids, that have bombarded spacecrafts on all space ventures. In order to study these particles, scientists prepared special surfaces to be exposed to space. Smooth gold-covered plates roughly six inches square with layers of film enclosed within them were exposed for 72-hour periods during both manned and unmanned flights. When the particles struck, they left small craters in these surfaces. By examining the craters, scientists learned the mass, size, and velocity of the space particles.

Other mapping experiments were designed to survey the sky and determine the many sources of energy in the universe.

Teenage Contributors

The Skylab experiments were for the most part devised by NASA and universities. But not all of them. NASA had an idea. Why not rekindle dwindling American teenage interest in space with a Skylab experiment contest? The contest was announced, more than 80,000 applications were made, and there were more than 3,400 actual entries, from which NASA picked 25 winners. Of these, 19 actually became part of the flight plan. The breadth of these experiments was exciting. In one, the web formation of spiders in zero gravity was compared with web formation on earth. In another, the growth of radishes on Skylab was compared with that of radishes planted on earth. In other experiments, ultraviolet rays from quasars and ultraviolet light from pulsars were studied. And in still another experiment, bacteria and spores were grown in Skylab and photographed regularly, and bacteria, spores, and photographs were later returned for earth evaluation.

Whether the Skylab astronauts looked outward toward interplanetary space or downward toward earth, the view was one of the longest and best man had ever had. It whetted the appetites of scientists for even more information. Increasingly sophisticated space stations will probably appear in the 1980s to carry on the pioneer work of the first three-man crews of Skylab.

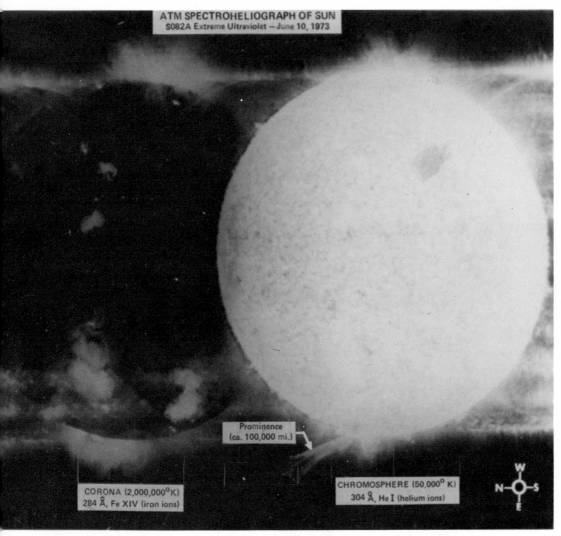

This spectroheliograph of the sun was taken by Skylab's Apollo Telescope Mount on June 10, 1973. Skylab's telescopes took pictures of solar flares never before photographed in such close detail.

The Men of Skylab

The nine astronauts who made up the Skylab crews had trained, prepared, and just plain waited for their trips for a long time. All the men were with the U.S. manned space program for at least seven years, and two were with it for over a decade. Only two of the nine were space veterans. In fact, the third crew consisted entirely of space rookies!

Crew Composition

Early plans for crew composition ranged from having all pilots to having all scientists. NASA's final decision, one that would show the most profitable return of information from the mission, was to compose each crew of two military pilots and one scientist. These designations were not as clear-cut as the titles would suggest, though. When originally selected for the space program, the pilots were chosen largely on the basis of their military flying experience, and the scientists were picked because of their background in particular scientific areas. However, after years of training and study, the pilots became competent scientific researchers, and the scientists not only broadened their scientific backgrounds but became proficient pilots.

It is often asked why flight training was an imperative for the astronaut program and why military pilots predominated in the crew rosters. The answer is simple. On any spaceflight, events that could affect the success of the mission or even the survival of the crew could take place in times measured in milliseconds. Time was a luxury the astronauts did not have; they had to be prepared to act almost automatically. The only place now known where men could gain the experience necessary for such snap decisions was in high-speed aircraft under combat or under test-flight conditions. Simulators had their place, but mistakes made in them were not of vital importance; a test could always be run again. But in space, or in a jet, the decision had to be right the first time. Thus, flight training was the perfect school for building up the confidence and competence the astronauts needed, and it showed as well whether the astronaut-students had what it took to become proficient astronauts.

It is also often asked why a physician was not included on every flight to handle emergencies and to take care of problems that could cut the mission short. But that just was not feasible, restricted as the flights were to three crew members and with the aims of the missions being the gathering of solar information, earth resources information, and life sciences information. Further, considering the superb physical condition of the astronauts, there was a better chance that one of the scientists could save the mission by fixing a piece of equipment than that a doctor would save it by mending a body.

Duties of the three-man crews were distributed according to the men's backgrounds and abilities. The mission commander's specialties were the launch of the Command/Service Module, rendezvous and docking, extravehicular activities, and de-orbit and reentry into the earth's atmosphere. The science pilot's specialties were the Apollo Telescope Mount system, extravehicular activities, and medical experiments. And the pilot's specialties were the Airlock Module, the Multiple Docking Adapter, and the Orbital Workshop systems and the earth resources experiments.

The First Crew

Commander of the first Skylab crew was Navy Captain Charles "Pete" Conrad, Jr., a real space veteran, who brought to the Skylab program an amazing 506 hours and 48 minutes of actual spaceflight experience, of which 7 hours and 45 minutes were spent outside on the lunar surface.

Pete Conrad entered the astronaut program in September 1962 and made three spaceflights before Skylab. In August 1965, as pilot of the eight-day Gemini 5 mission, he along with Command Pilot Gordon Cooper established what was then a space-endurance record of 190 hours and 56 minutes in orbit, covering a total of 3,312,993 statute miles, thus giving the United States the lead in man-hours in space. In September 1966, this time on Gemini 11, he successfully docked with an unmanned Agena spacecraft and piloted Gemini 11 while his partner, Richard Gordon, walked in space. A highlight of Pete's career will probably always be the Apollo 12 mission, in which he was the third man to set foot on the moon. With a play on Neil Armstrong's famous words when he stepped to the lunar surface, smallish Pete said, "Man, that may have been a small step for Neil, but that's a long one for me." He then let out a "Whoopee" as he pranced around the lunar surface.

Experienced jet pilots, the astronauts used T-38 jet trainers for training and for commuting between the John F. Kennedy Space Center in Cape Kennedy, Florida, the Lyndon B. Johnson Space Center in Houston, Texas, and the Marshall Space Flight Center in Huntsville, Alabama. Charles Conrad is seated in the near aircraft. Joseph Kerwin and Paul Weitz occupy the cockpits of the far craft.

November, 1969. Charles Conrad is shown with Surveyor 3. In the distance is the Apollo 12 Lunar Landing Module.

Hawk nosed, balding, standing 5 feet 6½ inches, Captain Conrad is the smallest of the astronauts sent into space. His personality is outgoing, and one of his astronaut friends has remarked of him: "Pete never met a stranger." The kind of leadership he provided for the crew of Skylab can probably best be summed up in the words of Dr. Joseph Kerwin: "We looked to Pete for leadership, and he kind of took us there imperceptibly."

Flying has always been the center of this astronaut's life. He recalls wanting to build and fly airplanes even as a youngster and at 14 worked at a nearby airport to earn money for flying lessons. He soloed after only eight hours of instruction—the minimum required. After his 1953 graduation from Princeton University (the only eastern university at that time offering courses in aeronautical engineering), he entered the Navy and spent most of his early career as a test pilot. He has logged over 6,000 hours of flight time, primarily in jet planes. As if that were not enough, he has also raced boats and motorcycles and presently drives in automobile races, placing as high as third against professionals. In the course of all these activities, he has accumulated a warehouseful of honors, trophies, and medals, ranging from a string of honorary degrees to an award for lunar photography from the National Academy of Television Arts and Sciences, the group that presents the coveted "Emmy." His other interests include golf, swimming, water skiing—and country music. The country-and-western music cassettes aboard Skylab were there by his choice.

Captain Conrad was born in Philadelphia, Pennsylvania, June 2, 1930, and he and his wife, Jane, have four sons.

The second member of the crew and the science pilot was Commander Joseph P. Kerwin. He is unique in that he is both a medical doctor and a fully qualified Navy jet jockey. The first U.S. doctor to go into space and the only one to fly in the Skylab program, Dr. Kerwin was there to make on-the-spot observations of the effects on the men of a long-duration spaceflight. His secondary duty was to take care of the crew's medical needs and any inflight medical emergencies. He is a graduate of Northwestern University Medical School and also attended the U.S. Navy School of Aviation Medicine at Pensacola, Florida. Dr. Kerwin has been in the Navy Medical Corps since 1958, earned his pilot's wings in 1962, and has logged 2,000 hours of flying time. He was selected as an astronaut in 1965.

Dr. Kerwin is as handy with a pair of pliers as he is with a stethoscope. He completely wired his house for a room-to-room stereo system and put in an entire yard sprinkler system. The off-duty recreation materials he took into space with him tell something more about him —a short history of the United States, a book of poetry, and tape cassettes including, among other composers, Shostokovitch.

Joseph Kerwin was born in Oak Park, Illinois, February 19, 1932, the seventh of eight children. He and his wife, Shirley, are the parents of three daughters. Of his daughters' reaction to his Skylab assignment, Dr. Kerwin said, "The big thing they know is that I'm not going to be around the house for two months."

Completing the all-Navy crew was Commander Paul J. Weitz, pilot for the mission. He has been an astronaut since 1966. Skylab was his first spaceflight, and his job was to keep the Command/Service Module in shape for its return to earth. In addition, Commander Weitz carried out many of the earth resources experiments. Although this was his first venture into space, flying high above the earth is a familiar experience for him, for he has accumulated almost 4,000 hours of flight time since winning his gold Navy wings in 1956.

As a naval pilot in 1965, he flew 120 combat missions in Southeast Asia, making it through without a scratch. Of those missions as compared to the Skylab assignment, he feels that "spaceflight is much safer." And of the force that drove him into the space program, he has said, "It's one of the few frontiers left. It takes a little more and not just everybody can go."

Commander Weitz is one of the quietest of the astronauts. His choice of spaceflight reading matter is revealing; stowed away in the Skylab library were Edward Fitzgerald's translations of the *Rubaiyat of Omar Khayyam*—all seven of them. He is an avid outdoorsman, and his special interests include hunting and fishing. In addition, according to his wife, who was not surprised that the three astronauts were able to repair the crippled Skylab, he can fix just about anything he puts his mind to.

Commander Weitz was born in Erie, Pennsylvania, on July 25, 1932. He is a 1954 graduate of Pennsylvania State University and earned his master's degree in aeronautical engineering in 1964 from the U.S. Naval Postgraduate School. He and his wife, Suzanne, are the parents of a son and a daughter.

The Second Crew

The second crew was commanded by Captain Alan Bean, another Navy man, whose background and achievements parallel those of Pete Conrad. Captain Bean has logged 4,410 hours in 27 different types of military aircraft as well as many different types of civilian aircraft. He was a Navy test pilot before he was chosen to become an astronaut in 1963. After entering the program, Captain Bean had to wait around for several years before taking his hoped-for trip into space. He was part of the backup crews for both the Gemini 10 and Apollo 9 missions. However, he did finally make it with Apollo 12, in November 1969, when he and Pete Conrad made a near pinpoint landing on the moon's Ocean of Storms in their Lunar Module, the *Intrepid,* to begin one of the most successful Apollo explorations. Ecstatic about being on the lunar surface, Captain Bean said, when it was time to return to the Lunar Module, that he would have liked to stay on the moon all day. Before the Skylab mission, Captain Bean had 244 hours 36 minutes of actual spaceflight experience, of which 7 hours and 45 minutes were spent outside on the moon's surface.

Captain Bean was born in Wheeler, Texas, March 15, 1932, and graduated with a degree in aeronautical engineering from the University of Texas in 1955. He and his wife, Sue, are the parents of a son and a daughter.

Science pilot for this crew was Owen K. Garriott, a civilian with a doctoral degree in electrical engineering from Stanford University. Dr. Garriott taught at Stanford before his selection as a scientist-astronaut in 1965. As part of his training, he went through the regular Air Force pilot training program at Williams Air Force Base in Arizona, where he won his silver Air Force wings. He now has more than 1,600 hours of flight time to his credit.

Dr. Garriott, who was born in Enid, Oklahoma, on November 22, 1930, pinpointed the beginning of his interest in space to an evening back in Enid. "When I was a youth," he said, "my dad, who was a chemist, asked me if I wanted to go along with him to a meeting of ham radio operators. You can trace my interest in engineering and science back to that one suggestion my father made." His off-duty interests include amateur radio, sailing, and scuba diving. He and his wife, Helen, are the parents of three sons and a daughter.

Pilot for the second launch was Marine Major Jack R. Lousma, a space rookie who entered the astronaut program in 1966. He is an experienced Marine pilot, with 2,600 hours of flight time to his credit. When the helicopters picked him up in the Pacific Ocean after his

Crew number two. Alan Bean, foreground, Owen Garriott, left, and Jack Lousma are here photographed in the Skylab mock-up at the Johnson Space Center in Houston, Texas.

tour of duty aboard Skylab, he felt right at home, for he is also a competent chopper pilot.

Major Lousma was born February 29, 1936, in Grand Rapids, Michigan. He is a 1959 graduate in aeronautical engineering from the University of Michigan and has a second degree from the U.S. Naval Postgraduate School. In his free time Major Lousma teaches Sunday school, and he took the *Book of Psalms* and the *Book of Proverbs* along for spaceflight reading. Explaining his choice of taped music, he said, "I'm not much of a classical man. I'm taking the William Tell Overture, but it's really the Lone Ranger to me." Major Lousma and his wife, Gratia, are the parents of two sons and a daughter.

At the end of the Skylab program, Major Lousma will move to the Apollo-Soyuz Test Project. He will, however, probably not get a chance to travel in orbit on this flight, for he is scheduled as backup docking pilot.

The Third Crew

The third crew was made up entirely of first-time space travelers. Two are military officers, and the third is a civilian with a Ph.D. degree in engineering.

Mission commander was Lieutenant Colonel Gerald P. Carr, an experienced Marine Corps pilot with more than 3,100 flying hours to his credit. He has been with the astronaut program since 1966, was a member of the support crews for Apollo 8 and 12, and played an important role in the development and testing of the lunar roving vehicle that was used to get around on the moon.

Lieutenant Colonel Carr has a degree in mechanical engineering from the University of Southern California, a degree in aeronautical engineering from the U.S. Naval Postgraduate School (1961), and a Master of Science degree in aeronautical engineering from Princeton University (1962). His interests include sailing, golf, tennis, woodworking, and the restoration of an old automobile.

Gerald Carr was born August 22, 1932, in Denver, Colorado, and grew up in Santa Ana, California, which he calls home. He and his wife, JoAnn, are the parents of three sons and three daughters, including two sets of twins.

Civilian Edward G. Gibson was the science pilot of the third crew. Dr. Gibson—he received his Ph.D. degree in engineering—was chosen for the astronaut program in 1965, and like Owen Garriott, had to go through the Air Force pilot training program at Williams Air Force Base in order to earn his wings. Since then he has flown both jet aircraft and helicopters, logging 1,500 hours of flight time. He served as

Space rookies made up the crew of the third manned mission. Commander Gerald P. Carr, center, is flanked by Science Pilot Edward G. Gibson on the left and Pilot William R. Pogue on the right. On the table are a dart board and darts—recreation equipment carried aboard Skylab.

part of the support crew for Apollo 12.

This astronaut's specialties are in the fields of engineering and physics. He has degrees from the University of Rochester (1959) and the California Institute of Technology (1960 and 1964) and is the author of a textbook entitled *The Quiet Sun.*

Dr. Gibson was born November 8, 1936, in Buffalo, New York. His interests range from athletics of all kinds to scuba diving and solar observation. He and his wife, Julia, are the parents of two daughters and a son.

Pilot for the last Skylab visit was Lieutenant Colonel William R. Pogue of the Air Force, who has spent a great deal of time in the

One backup crew supported the first Skylab Mission. However, only a single backup crew waited in readiness for both the second and third missions.

First Mission

Commander:
Russell Schweickart
Born 10-25-35, Neptune, N.J.

Science Pilot:
Story Musgrave, M.D.
Born 8-19-35, Boston, Mass.

Pilot: Bruce McCandless II,
Lt. Comdr., U.S.N.
Born 6-8-37, Boston, Mass.

Second and Third Missions

Commander: Vance Brand
Born 5-9-31, Longmont, Colo.

Science Pilot: William Lenoir
Born 3-14-39, Miami, Fla.

Pilot: Don Lind
Born 5-18-30, Midvale, Utah

cockpit of an airplane. He flew combat missions in the Korean War and spent two years in England on an exchange program with the British Royal Air Force, during which time he graduated from England's Empire Test Pilots' School and served as a test pilot with the RAF. He has been checked out in more than 50 different types of American and British aircraft and has logged 4,400 hours of flight time. He was a member of the U.S. Air Force's Thunderbirds, a precision-flying team.

William Pogue was born January 23, 1930, in Okemah, Oklahoma, and received his undergraduate degree from Oklahoma Baptist University. From 1960 to 1963 he taught math at the U.S. Air Force Academy. In 1966 Lieutenant Colonel Pogue entered the astronaut program and has since served on the support crews for Apollo 7, 11, and 14. His interests include squash, handball, and stereo systems. He and his wife, Helen, are the parents of two sons and a daughter.

NASA did something different in the way of backup crews for Skylab. Instead of one backup crew for each prime crew, one backup group supported the first launch and a single crew stood in readiness for both the second and third launches. This cut down on training time and expensive equipment such as the specially fitted space suits each man had to have. Assignment to a backup crew was undoubtedly one of the more frustrating duties for an astronaut, for while working to see that everything went as planned, he had to have some hidden desire to find a way to go along for the ride.

When the final crew undocked and left Skylab, it was certainly with a touch of sadness; anyone who had experienced the uniqueness of living aboard the orbiting space station would surely have come to feel some affection for it. And for some of the men, Skylab may have been their last chance to leave the bounds of earth.

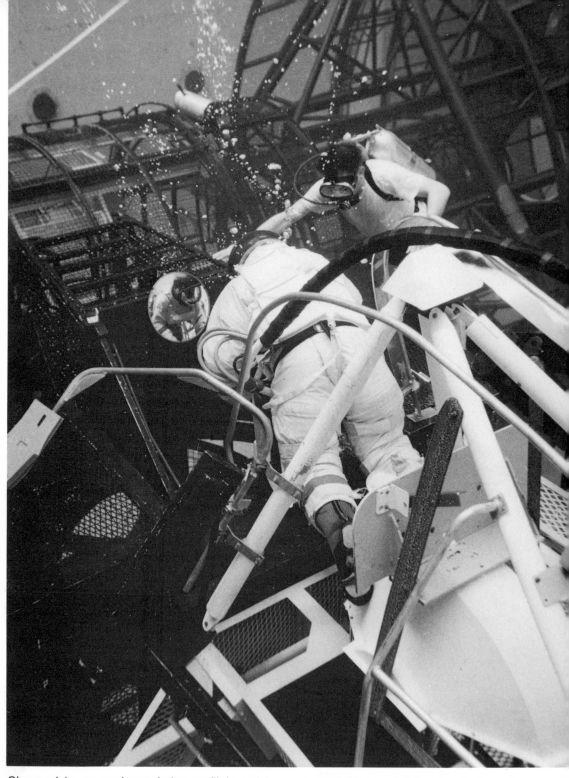

Observed by an engineer during preflight training, astronaut Gibson checked handrails and footholds atop the Apollo Telescope Mount. Scene was the Skylab mock-up in the neutral buoyancy simulator at the Marshall Space Flight Center in Huntsville, Alabama.

Getting Ready to Go

7

An astronaut must have the physical prowess of an athlete, the mental alertness of a Grand Prix auto racer, and the scholarship of a scientist. But to compete in the arena of space requires even more than native abilities and acquired knowledge. It requires months and even years of practice, training, and rehearsal. Thus, more than a year before the first launch of Skylab, the nine astronauts and the many ground personnel started final preparations for the upcoming trips. The rigid training and testing schedule was designed to familiarize the men with the job and the equipment they would handle in orbit as well as to catch any potential problems in the Skylab hardware.

Crew Training

Much of the training took place in the classroom. While each astronaut is an expert in his chosen field, the men still had much to learn from books, reports, and long hours of briefings.

In addition the men had to thoroughly understand the more than 20,000 pieces of equipment aboard the station. Because of the complexity of Skylab, it was necessary for the men to specialize to some degree in various areas of activity, although there was considerable crossover between areas of responsibility. One hundred percent cross-training was not possible, however.

The men got to know every nut and bolt of the space station and the Saturn launch vehicles, knowledge that could mean the difference between life and death during an in-orbit emergency. This detailed familiarity paid off both before and after launch. During the development of the program, the crewmen made several major contributions to the design of the spacecraft and helped make the multitude of technical decisions that occurred during the course of the program. This firsthand knowledge was crucial in making the many repairs that kept Skylab "alive."

To get their minds and bodies into shape, as well as to prepare them for the new sensations of space, the astronauts participated in a vigorous physical-training program. Running and handball were two of the most popular conditioning activities; since most of the men were physical-fitness nuts anyway, this part of the preparation was really fun and games. However, getting into condition for the high-gravity accelerations to come during the launch and reentry was a physical challenge of another kind. The men took rides in a whirling centrifuge. Seated in a compartment at the end of a girder, they were pressed back in their seats as the compartment was spun faster and faster.

Weightlessness was still another matter since it is nearly impossible to duplicate on earth. The best that could be done was a mere 20-or-so seconds of zero gravity during the high-lofting trajectory on a flight of the Air Force's KC-135 airplane, a specially modified version of the Air Force's jet tanker. As short as this weightlessness simulation was, the crewmen made good use of it. During flights they got the feel of being suspended in midair and were able to check out flight hardware and techniques.

The second best way to duplicate weightlessness while still attached to the earth happens in a surprising place. Under water. A man in a pressurized space suit loaded with properly sized weights neither rises nor sinks when he goes underwater. To make use of this similarity to weightlessness, NASA used a huge tank at the Marshall Space Flight Center in Huntsville, Alabama. Called the neutral buoyancy simulator, it held almost 1½-million gallons of pure water and looked much like the huge tanks at Sea World or Marineland. But it held no whales or porpoises. Inside there was almost an entire mock-up of Skylab. Both astronauts and engineers became experts in scuba diving after spending many hours in the tank. Space-experienced astronauts said that underwater weightlessness is very much like the real thing.

When the astronauts got a little too waterlogged, they could dry out during training on the desert. Both jungle- and desert-survival techniques were important parts of the Skylab preparation schedule. If for some reason the mission had to be aborted and the men went down in some remote part of the world, they had to be prepared to cope with primitive conditions until rescued.

Because of the tremendous cost of the mission, NASA did not want to run the risk of having to bring the men back early in case of minor illnesses or accidents. Thus, two members of each team were given extensive first-aid training. Except for Dr. Kerwin, they were not qualified to make extensive diagnoses, but they could report conditions to physicians who, by way of ground-to-orbit television, could take a look at the patient and tell the astronauts what to do. Using medical

Preflight training included tests of food to be consumed during actual missions. Here astronaut Charles Conrad prepares a meal in the wardroom of the Orbital Workshop.

supplies stowed aboard Skylab, the crewmen could perform operations even as complex as a tracheotomy or set a fracture and could prevent shock and stabilize the patient before coming down from orbit. The possible level of treatment was somewhat beyond what a doctor can administer in his office.

To get actual on-the-job medical training, the men worked in the emergency room of a Houston hospital, where they patched up wounds from auto accidents and Saturday-night fights. In anticipation of serious dental problems, they also practiced dental procedures, such as pulling teeth, in dental clinics at Lackland and Sheppard Air Force bases. The patients were enlisted men and officers who volunteered. Included among them was a retired Air Force general who waited two weeks to have a tooth pulled by an astronaut-dentist. The only complaint registered was by a patient who experienced some discomfort when one of the "dentists" forgot to take off his watch before extracting a tooth, and the watch pulled the man's hair.

As a precaution against illness in orbit, the astronauts participated in a special preflight health program. For 21 days preceding launch, they lived in crew quarters at the Lyndon B. Johnson Space Center in Houston and at the John F. Kennedy Space Center near the launch point. While confined to these quarters, they were isolated from carriers of sniffles, sneezes, and fevers, and their contacts were limited to a small group of people who were themselves constantly checked to make certain they were in good health and had not been in contact with people who were sick. During this time the astronauts also underwent a battery of medical tests. X rays, blood studies, and other laboratory tests reassured doctors about the state of the men's health and enabled them to establish baselines against which postflight studies could be checked.

During this preflight period, the men ate the same food they would be served in orbit and had a chance to rate it and express their preferences. NASA, too, had a chance to see if the food satisfied the crews' daily energy requirements and also to ascertain whether the food would disagree with the crews, who would have to live on it for months. Information was also gained which would contribute to the medical experiments that measured the men's food intake and body wastes while in orbit.

The Apollo Telescope Mount, with its many cameras, its humming electronics, and its rows of brightly lighted control panels, was a highly complicated piece of equipment and a challenge to the astronauts. They wanted to do more than just twirl knobs and read dials; they wanted to understand and interpret what they saw. Because of the complexity of the equipment and because the solar observations were such an important part of the mission, a program was designed to help the men become expert solar astronomers. Much of their training took place in the classroom, where a closed-circuit TV system was hooked up to a NASA solar telescope. The men also traveled around the country to observatories, where they worked with the telescopes and talked with practicing astronomers.

The design of such a complex "house" as Skylab involved the talents of thousands of engineers and designers, who produced tons of drawings that showed the layout in minute detail. From these, mock-ups were made of almost every part of the spacecraft. Of all the mock-ups, the most fascinating was the full-sized Orbital Workshop, which duplicated in almost every detail the complete interior of the actual workshop and was outfitted with models of all the flight hardware that would travel inside the real workshop. The realism was uncanny; the only element lacking was weightlessness. Astronauts moved between compartments, checked hatches and doorways for size, studied where every piece of equipment would be stowed, and worked out on the exercise equipment. In short, they familiarized themselves with the huge space workshop. Designs were tried out here, and changes made. Once a part worked to everyone's satisfaction, it was manufactured.

Aside from its function as a vital part of the Skylab program, the mock-up became one of the big tourist attractions in Huntsville, Alabama. Untold numbers of newsmen, teachers, students, and even Russian spacemen had a chance to examine the model. NASA probably should have charged admission and helped make a dent in the huge bill for Skylab!

One of the highlights preceding the actual launch was a two-month dress rehearsal in another mock-up Skylab Orbital Workshop at the Lyndon B. Johnson Space Center in Houston. Objectives of the experiment were manifold. Men, equipment, and procedures were all checked out, and extensive medical data on the men's reaction to confinement was collected for later comparison with similar data to be obtained while men were in orbit, with differences attributed to the effects of weightlessness.

In midsummer of 1972, astronauts Bob Crippen, Karol Bobko, and Dr. Bill Thornton entered the altitude chamber where the mock-up was located, not to emerge until late September. These two months inside the 20-foot chamber simulated in every way possible the actual conditions the astronauts could expect in their orbital journey. The men lived on the same food and water, breathed the same oxygen-nitrogen mixture, felt the same five-pounds-per-square-inch atmosphere, followed the same daily schedule, and even communicated

Thousands of practice sessions preceded the actual launch of Skylab. Astronauts Garriott and Lousma assist Alan Bean into his pressure suit.

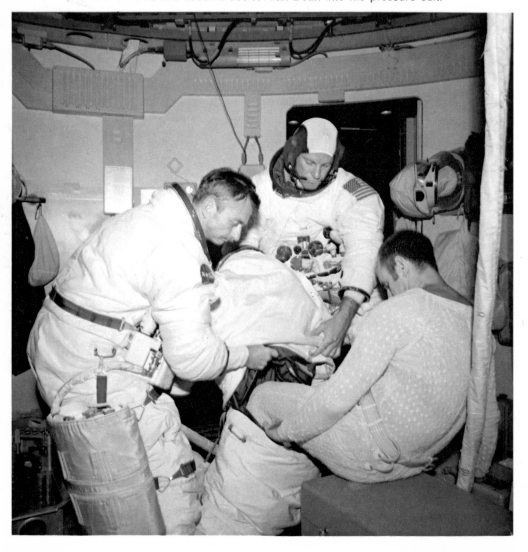

A cutaway view showing the "first floor" of Skylab. Roughly clockwise, the experiment compartment is at 12 o'clock, the wardroom at 5 o'clock, the waste management compartment at 6 o'clock, and the sleep compartment at 9 o'clock. Broom-closet-sized sleeping quarters are visible in the sleep area, and the unique food preparation table can be seen in the wardroom.

with the outside world with the same electronic gear to be used later in the orbiting Skylab. The men actually held a couple of press conferences, just as the Skylab astronauts would later do from space. The mock-up did not contain duplicates of the experiments to be contained in the finished space station, however, and the men had to find other activities to keep themselves busy. They did. They read a number of books, assembled some model cars, and worked on a course in Russian—probably thinking of the 1975 joint space mission with the Soviet Union.

When they emerged from the test, Crippen, Bobko, and Thornton were in good spirits and no worse for their experience. In fact, the

Preflight testing included evaluation of equipment to be used in the Skylab mission. Astronauts William E. Thornton, Karol Bobko, and Robert Crippen, participating in a series of experiments, spent eight weeks in an altitude test chamber at the Johnson Space Center in Houston, Texas. Medical data was also gathered during this session.

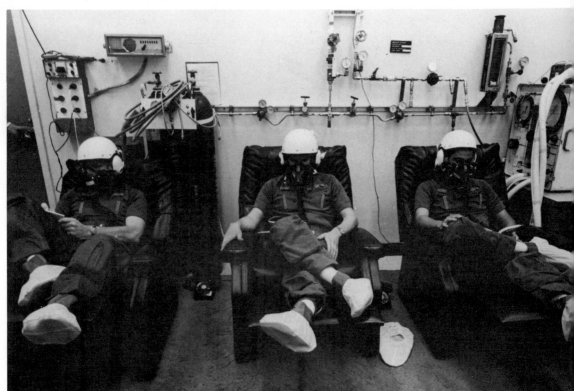

physicians who examined them thought they were possibly in better physical shape than when they entered the chamber.

Finally, both the prime and backup crews went through an 11-day exercise simulation of flight operations. Among other things, they found that the stowing of equipment between tasks was very difficult. The practice they got in the simulator would pay important dividends later in space.

In all, each crew member had in excess of 2,100 hours of training specifically geared to the Skylab mission. The training ranged from time spent in a variety of simulators, working with the experimental equipment and checking out the various systems, to first-aid training.

Ground-Crew Training

The orbiting astronauts were the men everyone got to know. However, another group of people equally important to the mission were the teams of ground controllers who followed the journey on video screens and control panels. Five complete teams kept a constant eye on the well-being of the men and the functioning of the hardware in Skylab.

Before launch the controllers were trained so that they knew every detail of the mission and the hardware inside and out. They read and often memorized piles of flight manuals, watched scores of videotapes, and listened to hours of briefings. They practiced not only the routine of the mission over and over again but also techniques to cover every eventuality and emergency so that they would be prepared to make the rapid decisions that might be required to save the mission or even the men. When the mission finally got underway, the controllers felt they had flown it many times before.

It is hard to conceive of the millions of hours of preparation that preceded the launch of Skylab. But on May 14, 1973, the Skylab team of astronauts, backup crew, and ground controllers was confident and ready for action. Their familiarity with every nut, bolt, heating or cooling coil, battery, dial, tool, and volumes of complicated instructions was to pay off handsomely. Had the team been less thoroughly prepared to cope with emergencies, the entire Skylab mission could have been aborted.

From its launch on May 14 until June 7, the giant laboratory limped along on minimal electrical power, its future uncertain. On the latter date, astronauts Charles Conrad (in background, with cable cutters) and Joe Kerwin (foreground) succeeded in freeing the workshop's remaining solar power wing. Instantly needles swept across indicator dials on the control panel: adequate electrical power was present. Skylab was, at last, functionally "go." The above on-the-spot photo was taken by astronaut Paul Weitz through a window in the Airlock Module.

Skylab in Orbit

As the launch date approached, the pace at Cape Kennedy quickened. For while all sections of the United States had had a hand in bringing Skylab to life, America's spaceport had the crucial job of putting the pieces together and starting the space station on its journey. The bulk of preflight activities occurred at the same facilities used for the moon landing program. Launch Complex 39, with its twin launch pads and Vehicle Assembly Building (the VAB), was once again in action.

Assembly of Skylab

As the pieces of the space station arrived by land, air, and water, they were delivered to the gigantic VAB. There, engineers and technicians, like a group of worried mothers, checked and rechecked everything. Huge overhead cranes crept along, stacking the many parts of Skylab into the launch configuration that would finally reach nearly 334 feet into the sky. At last they capped the launch vehicle with the Skylab Cluster, its upper part neatly packaged inside its shroud. As with the Apollo launches, the entire vehicle and its payload were assembled on the deck of the mobile launcher from which it would be sent aloft. Erection of Skylab began in September 1972, and on April 16, 1973, the mobile launcher carried the completely assembled vehicle to Pad A of Launch Complex 39, a distance of about 3½ miles. At the launch pad, it was ready for fueling, more checks, and the final countdown.

Movement of the Saturn V and its payload aboard the mobile launcher was an unbelievable sight, a little like seeing the Washington Monument sitting on a football field made of steel being pulled down a superhighway. The trip took 3½ hours, the slowest Skylab would ever travel; for in orbit it moved around the earth—a distance of 26,598 miles—a half-dozen times in a ten-hour period.

Past launches of the smaller Saturn IB took place from Launch Complexes 34 and 37, but these launch areas have since been scrapped. For the Skylab program, the Saturn IBs were launched from Pad B

The Orbital Workshop, a modified Saturn V third stage, moved into the Vehicle Assembly Building at the Kennedy Space Center in Cape Kennedy, Florida, eight months before launch. There it awaited mating with the launch vehicle.

of Launch Complex 39. Launch crews had a big job in preparing for the first and second launches, for this was the first dual countdown of a major launch program. Both the Skylab station on the Saturn V and the Command/Service Module on its Saturn IB, on their launch pads, were simultaneously going through the countdown procedures. Had Skylab 1 not experienced problems, Skylab 2, with its three-man crew, would have been launched 24 hours after the unmanned Skylab.

Some modifications were necessary so that Pad B could be used for the 100-foot-smaller Saturn IB. The most significant of these was the construction of a trusswork tower to hold the vehicle, making it look as though it was to be launched from stilts.

Since both the Saturn IB and the V use the S-IVB as the upper-most stage, elevation of the Saturn IB allowed use of the same service platforms for access to the S-IVB and the Command/Service Modules. The service platforms that normally serviced the Saturn V's second stage now touched the first stage of the Saturn IB.

Skylab in Trouble

To all appearances, the lift-off was perfect. With a thunderous roar and a trail of flames and smoke as it climbed through an overcast sky,

The workshop, here shown mated with the Saturn V launch vehicle. When complete, topped with the Skylab Cluster and the great nose cone, the structure would measure about 334 feet from tip to tail.

The Command/Service Module in which the astronauts would journey into space. The Service Module was installed in an altitude chamber where it was mated with the Command Module for preflight testing.

Skylab sped upward over the Atlantic Ocean. Spectators were jubilant. Everyone knew, or thought they knew, what was happening. The five-engined first stage completed its job and fell away. The second stage took over, pushing itself and the Skylab toward orbit. Only ten minutes after launch, Skylab arrived in orbit, the second-stage engines shut down, and the now-quiet second stage separated from the station and moved away. Minutes later, explosive charges peeled away the no-longer-needed protection of the Payload Shroud. That was what was happening, ground personnel knew, and they rejoiced in having seen the big bird perform the most trouble-free countdown and launch in its spectacular history. But their happiness was short-lived. Within the first hour after launch, data sent back to earth gave strong indications that all was not right aboard the orbiting space station.

As planned, the Apollo Telescope Mount pivoted into position, and its solar power wings unfurled. But even with repeated commands from the ground, the Orbital Workshop's two solar power wings, which were to supply about half the station's electrical power, failed to extend. Further, incoming data showed that the paper-thin aluminum shield designed to protect the craft from the sun's merciless rays and from micrometeoroids was gone. Skylab was in serious trouble. The interior of the Orbital Workshop would rapidly become too hot to live in, and it did not have sufficient electrical power to cool itself off or permit it to function as planned. Launch of the first crew, scheduled for the next day, was postponed. Pessimists were quickly calling Skylab a failure.

From telemetric data transmitted by the disabled vehicle, engineers began piecing together what had happened. The problems started only about 63 seconds after launch when air pressure built up under the micrometeoroid shield, forcing it away from the side of the space-craft where the supersonic airstream tore it away. In the process one of the solar power wings on the sides of the Orbital Workshop was lost altogether, and the other was locked in a closed position. The micro-meteoroid shield had a special thermal coating that protected the workshop from the sun's rays, helping to maintain a livable tempera-ture inside the space station. With the shield gone, temperatures on the outside surface of Skylab soared to over 300° F., and within hours the temperature inside started to rise, eventually reaching an average of 110° to 120°, and in some spots, an unlivable 190°.

The troubles compounded. Overheating in the space station began to affect the urethane insulation, which gives off deadly gases when temperatures rise above its tolerance. Some of these vapors are so lethal they can kill even in very low concentrations. Further, the con-tents of the space station were in danger from the intense heat. From actual testing and from discussion with drug manufacturers, it was

Above, riding smoothly aboard a modified mobile launcher, the Saturn IB left the Vehicle Assembly Building.

Arrived at Pad B of Launch Complex 39, the Saturn IB, at right, awaited the arrival of the first crew.

determined that as much as half the drug supply aboard Skylab would be ruined. Some of the food would also be affected by the high temperatures.

Engineers had two big problems to overcome, then, if any of the planned benefits were to come from the more than $2½ billion Skylab venture. They had to find a way to cool the station down. And they had to find ways to generate the power necessary to carry out the many experiments that were the reasons for Skylab's being.

All NASA centers involved with the program went on around-the-clock schedules, as did their contractors in the aerospace industry. Even technical people not on the Skylab team volunteered help and suggestions. Impossible tasks were performed in record time, and miracles became routine. The Skylab crews and their backup crews participated, too. Nobody wanted a promised trip into orbit to be scrubbed.

Answers for Some Problems

The electrical power crisis turned out to be, at least for the time being, the lesser of the two problems. The Apollo Telescope Mount's solar power array was in good working order, capable of supplying nearly

Launch Complex 39, Pad A. The Orbital Workshop atop the modified Saturn V, which would lift it into earth orbit. The complex Apollo Telescope Mount is hidden within the protective Payload Shroud.

10,500 watts of power for operating the space station and charging the batteries when the solar power wings were not in sunlight. When a Command/Service Module docked with the Skylab, its twin fuel cells would be able to provide more than 1,400 watts of electricity. One problem here, though, was that the Command/Service Module's fuel cells would be able to operate only for about 13 days before their supply of oxygen and hydrogen would be depleted. Then the Command/Service Module would have to draw about 1,200 watts of electricity from the Skylab system in order to keep in condition for the trip home. But by budgeting power and curtailing some of the high-energy-consuming experiments, NASA officials felt the Skylab mission could be carried out, at least on a limited basis, if the temperature in the cabin could be reduced. This was a big if!

Ground controllers managed to regulate the workshop's heat to some extent by shifting it around so that the forward, or docking end, faced the sun, thus exposing less of Skylab's surface to direct solar radiation. However, this move also directed the solar power wings on the Apollo Telescope Mount away from the sun, making them useless for generating electricity. Maneuvers of the great spaceship also drained the limited rocket-fuel supply. Obviously such maneuvers had to be executed only after careful weighing of alternatives. Nevertheless, with the shift in attitude, temperatures in the cabin did begin to decrease.

It was obvious, though, that some kind of sun shield was needed to replace the one that had been lost. All available engineers and technicians were put to work. Various NASA centers and several industry engineering teams brainstormed ideas and devices. Suggestions ranged from giant blankets to inflatable balloons to a large window-shade device that would be pulled down over the damaged area. The deadline, even with an extension from May 20 to May 25, seemed an impossible one. In the 11 days between the launch of Skylab and the launch of the first crew, the devices had to be designed, constructed, tested, and the astronauts trained in how to attach them to the orbiting space station. And yet, when the Saturn IB was at last launched, tucked away in the Command/Service Module were three different sun shields that would be able to do the job.

The two space sun shields carried into orbit as backups had the distinct disadvantage of requiring space walks to place them into position. The primary sun shield was a parasol-like device to be deployed through a scientific airlock on the sun side of the Orbital Workshop. The parasol fit into a standard canister that usually held experiments to be conducted through the scientific airlocks. It had a canopy of lightweight and reflectorized space-age materials and was supported by four telescoping booms. To erect the sun shield, the astronauts would place the canister into an airlock, would insert seven four-foot-

Skylab was in trouble. All NASA centers worked around the clock, pinpointing difficulties, searching for answers. Above, flight controllers and officials gather around Flight Director Donald Puddy's console at the Johnson Space Center in Houston, Texas.

Above right, Skylab in earth orbit. The parasol shield, erected by the first crew, shades the workshop in place of the missing micrometeoroid and heat shield. The single remaining solar power wing has been successfully deployed. Photo was taken during their final fly-around inspection by the first crew who then headed for home.

The canopy portion of the sun shield designed to take the place of the damaged micrometeoroid and heat shield. Shown at right, almost fully extended, the so-called parasol measured 22 by 24 feet. One of several versions tested at the Johnson Space Center in Houston, Texas, it was carried into space by the first crew.

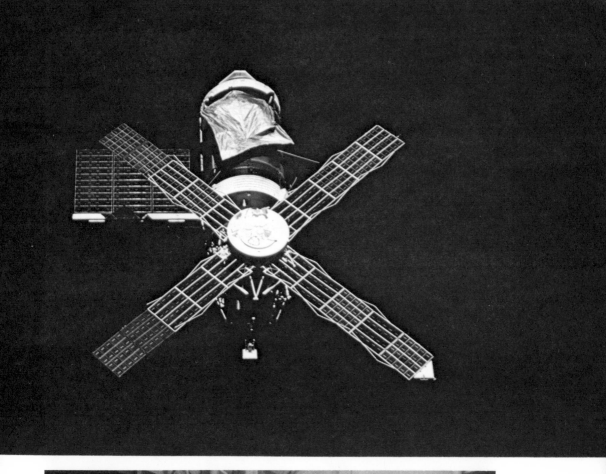

long poles into the canister, and would then push the parasol out into space. When the poles had extended the hub of the canopy 21 feet, the telescoping booms would clear the airlock. Internal springs would snap the four booms, with the lightweight material attached, outward to form a large X. The poles would be pulled back into the workshop until the canopy was only a few inches away from the surface of Skylab, and the poles would then be removed.

Interestingly, the division of NASA's Lyndon B. Johnson Space Center that came up with the parasol solution was headed by Pete Conrad's neighbor, Jack Kinzler. While not formally asked to develop a shield, Jack's group was called upon to make parts for the other solar shields. When it became apparent how difficult and dangerous it would be to place a solar shield during a space walk, Jack began to sketch a device that would eliminate the need for an extravehicular activity. When the correct-size aluminum tubing was not immediately available for a prototype of the device, Jack used a few $12.95 fishing poles from a local tackle shop to try out his idea.

While work on the sun shields progressed, solutions to other problems were also being sought.

To overcome the problem of the buildup of potentially deadly gases in the space station, ground controllers changed the air inside several times as the temperatures slowly went down.

The Command Module was altered for the repair mission. Lower priority items and experiments were removed to make room for some 400 pounds of tools and supplies that would be needed for the job of getting the Skylab mission back on course. New film and drugs to replace those destroyed by the heat were loaded aboard, and room was found for gas detectors and masks, binoculars, and additional film to use during the exploratory excursion around the crippled space station. Room had to be found for the sun shields and for the tools Paul Weitz would use in trying to free the damaged solar power wing during the first fly-around. Finally, the Command/Service Module had to be equipped so that the crew could live in it for five or more days if it turned out that they could not inhabit the Orbital Workshop.

The astronaut corps really got a workout prior to the launch. Kerwin, Weitz, and Conrad, as well as the other prime and backup crews, participated in most of the planning for the repairs that would rescue the ill-fated Skylab program. In mock-ups and simulators, they tried equipment and techniques that had not even been thought of a week or so before. One of the busiest places during this ten-day period was the oft-used neutral buoyancy simulator at the Marshall Space Flight Center. Here the men practiced underwater the many tasks, including the various space walks, they would have to perform under weightless conditions.

Astronauts Russell Schweickart and Story Musgrave of the first backup crew here do an underwater test on a proposed solar shield for the sunbaked Skylab. Erection of the shield would have required a hazardous space walk, however, and it was bypassed in favor of a parasol which could be deployed through a scientific airlock.

The Launch of Skylab 2

On May 25, 1973, Conrad, Kerwin, and Weitz finally boarded the patiently waiting Command/Service Module atop the Saturn I B. The sun shields just made it in time and were placed aboard a mere five hours before lift-off. The parasol was stowed away under Dr. Kerwin's couch.

This was the first launch of a Saturn I B in 4½ years, but the old bird performed just as expected. It placed the Command/Service Module into an elliptical orbit of 81 by 190 nautical miles. The rocket engine in the Service Module then raised the Command/Service Module to the 235-nautical-mile-high circular orbit of Skylab. The rocket engine was fired twice to get the Command/Service Module into phase with Skylab, reaching orbit at the precise point where the station was located. The 15,000-pound-thrust Service Module engine provided small bursts of power for making corrections along the way, for spiraling in on Skylab, and for braking the Command/Service Module as it neared its target. Rendezvous with Skylab occurred over Guam, and as ground controllers described it, was "nominal." However, the rest of that day in orbit was not.

Moving in on the station, the astronauts assessed the damage. Pete Conrad's description confirmed that the micrometeoroid shield had been completely stripped away and that it had taken one of the Orbital Workshop's solar power wings with it. The second wing was prevented from extending by a piece of the micrometeoroid shield jammed under it. The crew thought they could free the wing. But this would require a stand-up extravehicular activity; that is, wearing pressure suits and working through an open hatch, but remaining inside the Command/Service Module, they would attempt to remove the stubborn piece of debris.

Whenever possible, the men sent TV pictures back to the ground in real time so that ground controllers could update the detailed plans to repair the damage. The orbiting ships were often out of range of ground stations, though, so TV coverage was spotty. This was partly due to the fact that Skylab traveled in an orbit of greater inclination than previous manned flights. For economy reasons NASA was not able to build new tracking stations. The gap in coverage was a problem at times because ground personnel could not receive critical flight data on a real-time basis and thus were hindered in giving commands to control Skylab. Whenever TV pictures were available during the initial fly-around, they were shared with the general television audience so that the public got to see in real time the same things Conrad, Weitz, and Kerwin were seeing.

The Command/Service Module docked temporarily with Skylab, and the crew ate lunch. Meanwhile ground engineers determined that the material jamming the solar power wing could not be cut away with the tools aboard the Command/Service Module and that the astronauts would have to try to bend it out of the way. This information was relayed to the crew just as they were putting on their space suits.

Attempts to free the wing were futile. While Pete Conrad steered the Command/Service Module as close to the disabled Skylab as he dared, Joe Kerwin hung onto Paul Weitz's legs, and Weitz, using an improvised tool, leaned out of the open hatch and worked at the stubborn piece of metal. The men's frustration could be gathered from the profanity they used, the strongest to come from space yet—a probably not unexpected reaction from a crew of Navy veterans working a difficult problem with no success. They finally had to give up, only to find they were facing still another complication.

The plan was to move around Skylab to the Multiple Docking Adapter and to make a hard dock with the cluster, remove their space suits, and eat again. After three attempts to dock the Command/Service Module with the cluster, Conrad still could not get the two ships to mate. He sarcastically told ground controllers to stop feeding failures to the spacecraft, a reference to the many times the simulator operators had injected failures into the simulators so that the crew could get practice in handling unusual situations. After the third attempt, Conrad said he wanted to wait until Skylab was in darkness because navigation lights would then aid in guiding the two crafts together. After several more attempts, he sent word that docking had been accomplished and asked if the crew could get some sleep. They had been awake for 22 grueling hours and had big jobs in store for them. Mission Control told them to go to bed.

The crew slept soundly for the next seven hours and awoke fresh and ready to go again. Paul Weitz was the first to enter Skylab. Wearing a mask and using a sensor, he floated into the Multiple Dock-

Under water in the neutral buoyancy simulator, backup astronaut Russell Schweickart evaluated various tools and techniques for use by the first crew in freeing the jammed solar power wing. Here he tests a bone saw.

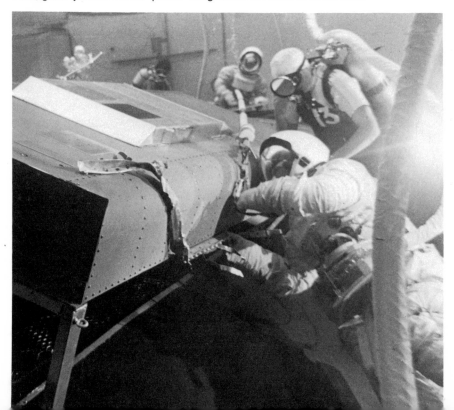

ing Adapter to check for dangerous gases and found that none were present. He then entered the Orbital Workshop, started the air-circulation fans, and made a quick inspection of the compartments. The heat, he said, was like that on the desert in summer, but it was not unbearable nor was anything hot to the touch. Pete Conrad then entered the workshop and found the only debris—a lost nut and a speck of red lint floating around. Then, while Dr. Kerwin watched from a window in the Command Module and sent TV pictures of the action to the ground, Conrad and Weitz began to deploy the parasol sun shield through the workshop's sun-facing airlock. The task went slowly but routinely.

The canister was installed in the airlock, and then the men waited until Skylab came into sunlight again before pushing the rods out and deploying the shield. When the rods had reached their limit, the parasol sprang into shape, although not entirely as planned. Instead of spreading out to a smoothly rectangular 22 by 24 feet, it was trapezoidal in shape and had several wrinkles. The shield was pulled in close to Skylab's surface, and this action along with subsequent baking by the sun smoothed it out somewhat.

With the deployment of the shield, temperatures started to drop and eventually leveled out at a relatively mild 80-or-so degrees, about 10 degrees higher than originally intended. The mission had taken a turn for the better, and it looked as though a 28-day stay aboard the space station might be possible.

For the first few days, temperatures in the workshop were still too high for the men to work there continuously. Periodically they retreated to the cooler Multiple Docking Adapter for a "heat break." In between they prepared the space station for the rest of the mission. In space terminology they put it into the proper "configuration"; that is, they moved equipment from launch position into the racks intended for it. There was some difficulty here, since heat had caused some of the equipment racks to warp, and the equipment modules did not slip effortlessly into place as planned. Nevertheless, everything was finally stowed away. Heat in the workshop declined steadily, and five days after launch of the Command/Service Module, the men were able to move into the workshop and actually live there.

The space station was still operating on limited electrical power, and use of electricity was carefully budgeted. A space walk, the most dangerous in history, would be required to free the jammed solar power wing. This space walk was postponed until later in the mission when the men would have, so to speak, their space "sea" legs.

In the meantime, the astronauts began concentrated work on the experiments, which were the primary reasons for Skylab's existence. With cameras and sensors, they recorded information about large swatches of the landscape that passed below them. They watched as hurricane Ava brewed 700 miles off the coast of Mexico and recorded the pollution entering San Francisco Bay and Lake Erie. They inspected crops growing in many parts of the United States and in distant parts of the world as well. They searched for oil and coal deposits in Mexico and studied faults in the earth's surface that could be hiding rich mineral deposits or could someday lead to major earthquakes. With their cameras they photographed urban sprawl in a dozen major U.S. cities. In all, they collected enough data to keep some 100 scientists—almost a quarter of them in other countries—busy for a long time.

With the powerful telescopes of the Apollo Telescope Mount, they were able to record events on the sun never seen by man. One of the most significant pieces of data to come from the entire mission was the observation for the first time in space of a major solar flare, an eruption of radiation from the upper solar surface and probably one of the sun's most spectacular phenomena. During such an event, great amounts of material are hurled into space, and enormous amounts of energy are released—in fact, more energy than is created by all man-made devices combined. Radiations from such outbursts disrupt long-range radio communications on earth and cause magnetic storms, which have been known to cause power blackouts. Study of solar flares has always been inhibited by the effects of the earth's atmosphere. But Skylab's superb cameras, above the atmosphere, recorded the eruption in great detail. With this new information, scientists hope to learn enough about solar flares to devise means of accurately predicting them.

Manufacturing experiments were carried out in the 16-inch-diameter work chamber. Metals were brazed and welded. Quarter-inch nickel spheres were formed. And other highly technical experiments were conducted.

Medical tests were also carried on, with Dr. Kerwin testing the men's ability to adapt to and work in space.

Freeing the Solar Power Wing

If Skylab were to accomplish most of its objectives, more electrical power was needed, and the only way to obtain it was to extend the remaining solar power wing from the side of the Orbital Workshop. In their first attempt to extend the solar power wing, the crew had been hindered by the lack of proper tools. On their second try, they would make use of tools carried in the Orbital Workshop to cut the obstinate two-foot-long strip of aluminum that was holding the wing in a locked position.

Skylab as seen by the first crew in their fly-around inspection. The micrometeoroid and heat shield is missing. At left, exposed cables show site of the lost solar power wing. At right, the remaining damaged, unextended wing.

A closeup view of the trouble. A thin but tough strip of aluminum prevented Skylab's one remaining solar power wing from extending freely. The strip was later cut and the wing deployed, giving the workshop more electrical power.

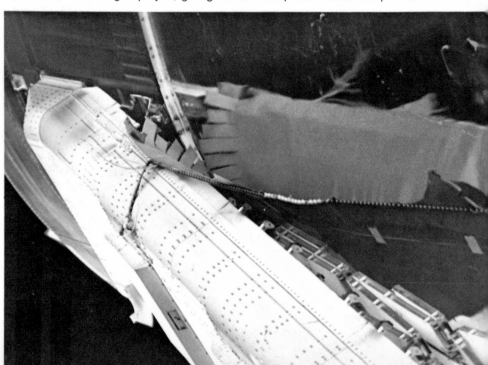

In-orbit "ballet." Dr. Joseph Kerwin demonstrates the wonder of weightlessness in the forward compartment of the Orbital Workshop. Above picture was beamed to earth via TV.

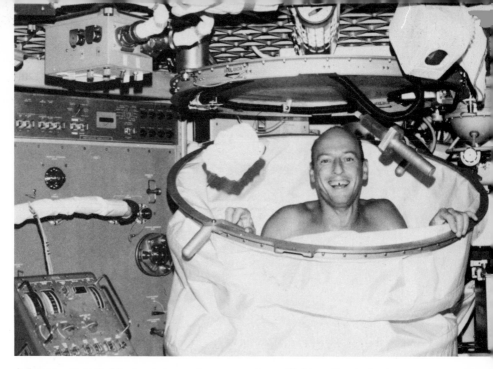

A luxury unavailable to astronauts on previous flights—the hot shower. Here Charles Conrad demonstrates the shower enclosure which lifts from the floor to connect with the ceiling. Crewmen expressed dissatisfaction with the facility, however, and have suggested reevaluation before use on any future missions.

On June 7, 1973, Conrad and Kerwin exited into space while Weitz monitored their actions from inside the space station. Their tool was a 25-foot aluminum tube, a rope, and a cable-cutting tool. The tubing was assembled outside the spaceship from five separate pieces. One end of the tube was fastened to the truss structure on the Apollo Telescope Mount. Then, using the pole as a handrail, Pete Conrad made his way up to the solar power wing. It took a great deal of persistence to maneuver the long pole so that the cutter was placed on the metal strip, but the pair finally managed to do it. Kerwin, at his end of the pole, then simply used the rope fastened to the pole to close the jaws of the cutter. Just in case this had not worked, Pete Conrad carried with him a bone saw from Skylab's medical supplies!

Once the aluminum strip was removed, Conrad had the job of extending the wing, whose working mechanisms had become frozen in the cold environment of outer space. He attached a rope between the wing and a strut on Skylab. Then, crouching with his feet against the side of the spacecraft and his shoulder under the rope, he pushed upward. By applying about 100 pounds of muscle power, he was able to break the mechanism loose, and the solar power wing extended. The "Fix Anything" crew, as it had become known, had triumphed again. With the solar power wing in operation, electrical power aboard Skylab nearly doubled, and everyone was optimistic that not only would the 28-day mission be completed but that the following two Skylab missions would also come off as planned.

Living in Space

The men marveled at how easy it was to move around in the zero-gravity environment. Weightlessness, Conrad said, actually made their work easier. All of the astronauts seemed to derive a lot of enjoyment from floating around effortlessly, and they developed some tricks and games that can only be played in an orbiting space station. They found they were able to run footraces around the circular walls of the second-floor workshop, with flips, somersaults, and handsprings thrown in for good measure. Thus the "Skylab 500," as the crew called these races, was born. On one of their days off, they sent pictures back to earth showing their antics to the general public. They even played a little football. During their game they showed that if a ball were thrown perfectly straight under weightless conditions, it would not arc and fall but would continue to fly straight until it hit a wall.

Surprisingly, Skylab's sleep restraints did not present many problems. Conrad said it was possible to sleep in just about any position imaginable. But the crews did suggest that future space stations be provided with soundproof sleeping compartments.

There were other difficulties, too. The gridwork floors and the companion boots with the triangular wedges on the soles created some problems. The astronauts found that if they did not get the boots securely attached, the boots would slip out of the grids, and the men would float away, often ricocheting off the walls.

Eating was another problem area. Food bags broke, scattering the contents all over the wardroom, and slices of bread floated out of reach. And the menu, carefully planned to avoid monotony, was not as satisfying as expected. The first crew complained that after a few days everything tasted alike. The second crew carried aloft a hefty supply of catsup, garlic salt, onion salt, chili powder, and Tabasco sauce to add flavor to the food.

Hygiene also presented unexpected problems. The men quickly discovered that if they filled the trash bags too full, the bags would jam the trash airlock when they tried to deposit the refuse in the waste tank. Early overheating of the spacecraft had ruptured a great number of toothpaste tubes and hand-cream containers, rendering them

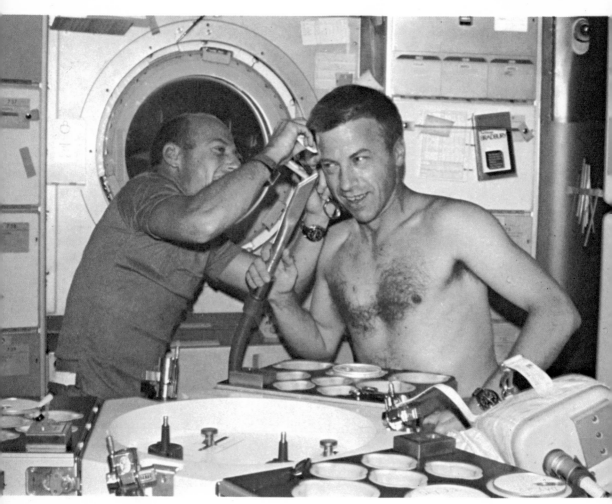

Photographed by Joseph Kerwin, Charles Conrad trims Paul Weitz's hair in the wardroom. Weitz holds a vacuum hose to collect free-floating hairs. In the background can be seen one astronaut's choice of space reading material, a book by science-fiction writer Ray Bradbury.

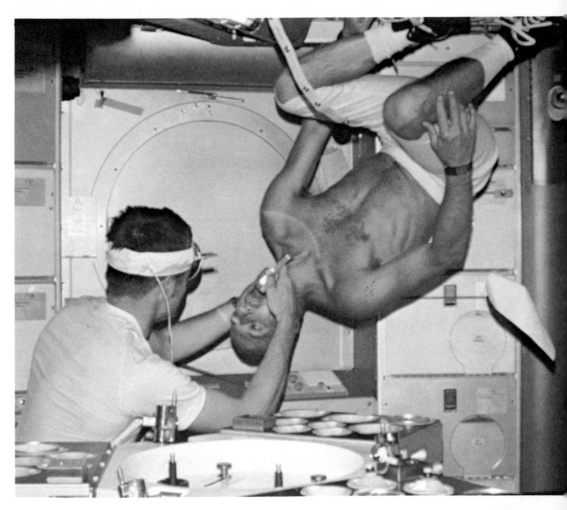

Astronaut Paul Weitz photographed Dr. Joseph Kerwin giving Charles Conrad an oral physical examination. Conrad, in the weightlessness of space, floats "upside down" with only a restraint around his left leg to hold him in position. Note the floating piece of paper at right.

useless. In the weekly showers, water tended to cling to the men's bodies and to the shower stall, and drying off took an extremely long time. And the blowers and other gear used in conjunction with the toilet made such a racket that it awakened any astronaut who happened to be sleeping at the time.

While the U.S. manned space program is amazing in its openness, there are times when privacy is needed, for example when a man wants to talk with his family or needs to consult a doctor. A ground-to-orbit communications link was set up for Skylab so that some conversations could bypass the press and all but a very small number of NASA officials. Highlights of the weeks in orbit for the men were their conversations with their wives and families. During the first flight, Pete Conrad's family wished him a happy 43rd birthday, and one of his sons, who is a budding pilot, asked his father's permission to go on a cross-country flight. The right to privacy was again invoked during a conversation Pete Conrad had with NASA doctors about his irregular heart action, which was determined not to be serious.

During the mission Pete Conrad became the astronaut with the greatest number of flight-hours in space. The previous record had been held by four-time space veteran James Lovell, who had accumulated some 715 hours in space. At splashdown Pete's new record surpassed Jim Lovell's by almost 20 days.

On the 24th day of the flight, the trio set a new record for manned spaceflight, later broken by the second crew. They surpassed the 23-day, 18-hour, 22-minute trip of the Russian Soyuz 11, the ill-fated flight that claimed the lives of three Russian cosmonauts when the hatch on their spacecraft failed just before the end of their record-setting space journey. Upon setting the new record, Pete Conrad asked either Donald "Deke" Slayton or Thomas Stafford to relay the Skylab crew's best regards to all the Russian spacemen and to wish them good luck on future Russian space trips. Slayton and Stafford are the two American astronauts who will join a Russian space crew in orbit during the planned 1975 Apollo-Soyuz Test Project.

In all, the first crew was able to complete more than 80 percent of the tasks scheduled for their flight, a pretty good accomplishment for a mission that looked like a total washout just weeks before.

Last Days of the First Flight

On June 19, 1973, Conrad and Weitz made the final space walk of the first Skylab mission, the only extravehicular activity that was actually planned for their flight. They replaced six canisters of film in the Apollo Telescope Mount's cameras. And here again the commander of the "Fix Anything" crew went into action. One of the telescope mount's batteries had a stuck switch. Conrad hit the battery with a hammer, hard enough to rock the whole Skylab. It did the trick. The battery immediately started to work, supplying 240 watts of needed electrical power. Conrad then proceeded to the solar telescopes, retrieved canisters containing over 30,000 priceless pictures of the sun, and passed them back to Paul Weitz, who was standing near the hatch. Pete then loaded the cameras with canisters of fresh film, and while at the telescopes, used a lens brush to clean away a speck of debris that was clouding the view of one of the instruments. Before going inside, he and Weitz also inspected the parasol sun shield and made suggestions as to how the next crew might make it work better.

In the last days of the flight, the crew tried out the automatically stabilized maneuvering unit, the Buck Rogers type rocket backpack that would be tested in the Orbital Workshop's upper story by a later crew. They found the backpack's thrusters made a lot of noise and suggested that ear protectors be worn and that everything loose be tied down before the firings. They also cleaned up the laboratory, fixed some pieces of equipment, and completed the final medical experiments.

Finally, on the last day, they packed the rolls of film and tape recordings, the body-waste samples, samples of drugs and foods, and their personal belongings into the waiting Command/Service Module. The last five hours before separation were spent in turning off the lights, adjusting the thermal-control system, and closing the hatch on Skylab. A problem arose with the craft's freezer system, which the crew was not able to fix and which, it was thought, would result in spoilage of some of the choicer foods such as lobster and steaks and which would also leave the craft without a place to store vital blood and urine samples. It was expected that the next Skylab crew would go aloft with a replacement freezer. However, the replacement proved unnecessary. For as mysteriously as the problem developed, it corrected itself. The second crew found food and biological supplies unharmed by the temporary rise in temperature.

After separation from Skylab, the men spent nearly an hour flying around the laboratory inspecting the solar arrays and the parasol and then headed earthward. Reentry, splashdown, and recovery were nominal. Shortly after the Command Module dropped into the Pacific Ocean 834 miles southwest of San Diego, helicopters dropped swimmers who attached a flotation collar and a sea anchor to the capsule. The aircraft carrier U.S.S. *Ticonderoga* maneuvered close to the capsule, and with a crane, lifted the famous spacecraft and its crew aboard. While the ship's band played "Anchors Aweigh," the triumphant trio walked unsteadily down 66 feet of red carpet. They immediately entered a trailerlike mobile laboratory for extensive medical examinations.

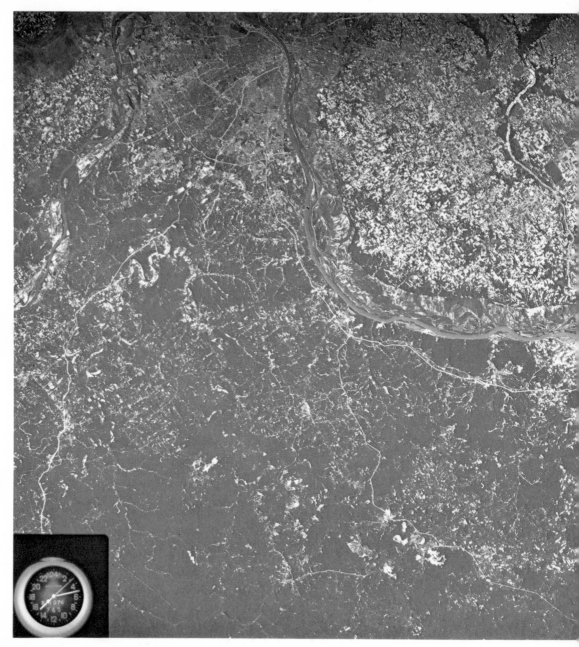

A space view of part of the United States. St. Louis, Missouri, and East St. Louis, Illinois, straddle (upper center) the Mississippi River, which cuts through the terrain in a southerly direction. The Skylab photos will make possible highly accurate mapping of large surfaces of the earth.

Return to Skylab

9

On July 28, 1973, a second trio of astronauts, on their way to live and work aboard the waiting Skylab, rode a Saturn IB through an overcast sky covering Cape Kennedy. This crew would remain in orbit an unprecedented 59 days. Like the first manned mission, this would be praised as an unqualified success. And again, like that mission, it would not be without its problems and moments of worry.

The final countdown of the Saturn IB carrying astronauts Alan Bean, Jack Lousma, and Owen Garriott had been so smooth that Jack Lousma fell asleep in the Command/Service Module about 45 minutes prior to launch and was not awakened until time for lift-off. But problems began to plague the crew almost as soon as they docked with Skylab and moved in. Most serious of these involved the Service Module itself. On August 2 it was discovered that two of the four small steering rockets on the Service Module had developed propellant leaks, and it was feared that the rockets would not be usable some two months hence when the Command/Service Module would have to be properly oriented during reentry. While there was no immediate danger to the crew, thought was given to having the astronauts return immediately while there was sufficient propellant to operate the failing rockets. The decision was made to proceed with the mission, however, and NASA started wheels rolling on its rescue option, just in case the men would not be able to make it back to earth on their own.

A thousand technicians and engineers went onto round-the-clock schedules. According to plan, the Saturn IB and Command/Service Module scheduled to ferry the third crew to Skylab was adapted for emergency use. Unneeded gear was stripped out of the Command Module and two extra couches installed. In the rescue configuration the Command Module could then carry—under rather crowded conditions—five astronauts. Astronauts Vance Brand and Don Lind were picked to pilot the rescue ship, which was to be ready for possible launch on September 5. The rescue spacecraft would dock at Skylab's main docking port after the ailing CSM was jettisoned, and the three Skylab astronauts could climb aboard for a cramped trip home.

But as with so many of Skylab's difficulties, the fuel leak problem was overcome, and the rescue craft was not needed. Fifty-nine days after launch, the original Command/Service Module returned home unaided. The Command Module splashed down within six miles of the prime recovery ship.

Unlike the first crew, all three men of the second crew experienced motion sickness during their first days in orbit. Their discomfort was so severe that many of the scheduled tasks and experiments had to be delayed, including a vital space walk to replace the film in the Apollo Telescope Mount and to erect a new solar shield. Concern was widespread. However, by about the fifth day into the mission the astronauts began to feel better and started working a full schedule. Shortly, during slack periods, they began catching up on work that had been postponed during those first days in orbit. And by the end of the mission they were working so efficiently that they not only completed most of their postponed tasks, but they kept ground controllers busy trying to find additional work for them to do. NASA officials have concluded that the trio ultimately exceeded the objectives of the flight by 150 percent.

The reason for the severe bout of nausea—and why all three men suffered from it—has puzzled the doctors. They have speculated that it may have resulted from the fact that the second crew moved directly from the confining Command/Service Module into the roomy weightless environment of Skylab immediately on reaching orbit; by contrast, the first crew spent some time in the CSM, even sleeping in it, before they entered and began bounding around in the workshop.

A host of creatures traveled into orbit with the second crew. On the passenger list were minnows, a pair of household spiders, a swarm of vinegar gnats, and half-a-dozen pocket mice. Unfortunately, early in the flight a power failure shut off the oxygen supply to the gnats and the mice, and the creatures died. The two minnows also died during the flight, but their offspring, the first births in space, survived the return to earth only to perish a day after touchdown.

Not since the early days of the space age have two nonhuman travelers enjoyed the fame of Arabella and Anita, the space spiders who were sent aloft to check their web-weaving ability under zero-gravity conditions. Arabella was the prime spider and Anita was the backup. Arabella was mightily confused in her first attempts at web spinning in space. Frantically she spun lines in all corners of her case. But Arabella adapted to the new environment. On the third day she spun a web that was more or less like one she might have spun on the ground. And on the 11th day Dr. Garriott noted that she had constructed a web that was essentially like one she might have woven in an earth-gravity environment. The astronauts shared fly-sized morsels of their filet mignon—served up rare—with the two spiders. Anita refused her share and starved to death before the end of the mission. Arabella thrived, however, and survived reentry, only to perish in her cage at Marshall Space Flight Center on September 28.

A new endurance record for space walking was set by astronauts Lousma and Garriott, once they were able to leave the space station. Their extravehicular activity on August 6 lasted just about 2 hours longer than planned, for an amazing total of 6 hours and 31 minutes— almost twice as long as the previous record set by the first crew. During their stay outside, they replenished the film in the Apollo Telescope Mount and repaired several of the experimental packages that were giving them trouble. The pair also erected the new solar

Most famous of nonhuman space travelers in recent years was the cross spider Arabella, who learned to spin her webs in a weightless environment.

shield engineers thought necessary because they feared the hurriedly made parasol erected during the first manned mission might not function properly for the remainder of the Skylab program. The twin-pole A-frame-mounted solar shield was placed above the original parasol. Installation took four hours, two hours longer than expected. With the new shield in place, temperatures inside the space station dropped into the 70s. During their 6½-hour space walk, the astronauts passed from daylight to darkness several times, pausing periodically in their work because of the lack of illumination. Even though the crew stayed outside so much longer than planned, there never was any uncertainty for their safety nor did any physiological problems arise.

Dr. Garriott was very excited about the solar observations made from the Apollo Telescope Mount. He found that even a "quiet" sun is an extremely dynamic sphere. The astronauts photographed two exceptionally large flares, one of which expanded over an area more than 17 times the diameter of the earth. The pictures—part of the immense amount of data that will probably keep several hundred

Astronaut Jack Lousma of the second crew is shown during a successful space walk. A major objective of this extravehicular activity was the deployment of a twin-pole solar shield over the parasol erected by the first crew.

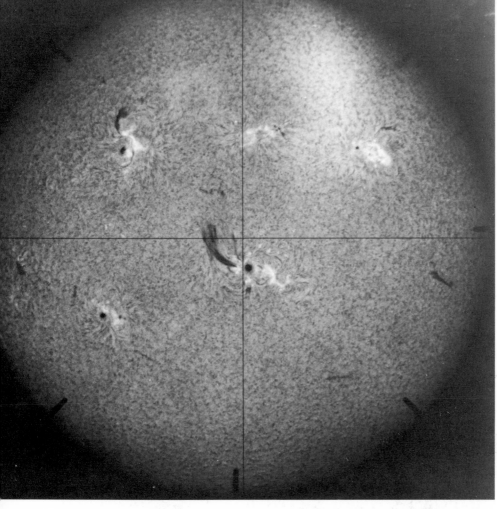

September 5, 1973. An alert astronaut, using the cameras in the ATM, caught an unusually large—and unexpected—sunspot and surge of gas.

solar scientists busy for several years—may contain clues to the cause of these mighty eruptions. The outbursts, so powerful that just one could generate all the energy the earth is likely to need in the next 500 years, were thought to be relatively rare before they were so frequently seen from Skylab. From the station, solar flares were observed about every two weeks, and the crew brought back pictures of about 100 flares.

Small glitches kept things interesting for the crew. There was even a false fire alarm. The shrill signal sounded one afternoon while Jack Lousma was conversing with mission control, causing excitement both in space and on the ground. The men investigated and found to their relief that there was no fire. The crew figured they spent about

Right. Fifty-nine days after launch, the second crew maneuvered their spacecraft back into earth's atmosphere. Main parachutes are here shown unreefing prior to splashdown.

Below. Back on earth, the crew was greeted by their wives; Dr. Donald K. Slayton; and Dr. Christopher Kraft, shown shaking hands with Pilot Jack Lousma.

1½ hours each day just troubleshooting. The problems they solved were usually relatively small, yet any of these could have put the whole mission out of commission if the men had not been on the spot to correct them.

The second Skylab mission saw Alan Bean become—for the time being—the world champion of spaceflight, surpassing the record set by his longtime friend Charles Conrad during the previous Skylab flight. Conrad's 28 days on the first manned Skylab mission, added to the 21 days he had previously logged on the flights of Gemini 5, Gemini 11, and Apollo 12, gave him a total of 49 days in space. Bean brought with him to Skylab a total of 10 days' space experience on Apollo 12. This, added to the 59 days of the second manned mission of Skylab, gave him an impressive total of 69 days spent in space. The record would stand only until astronauts Carr, Pogue, and Gibson surpassed it during the third manned mission. Their record is not likely to be broken by an American for some time to come.

A woman stowaway on Skylab? Things were running along smoothly, with the second mission nearing completion, when a female voice beamed down from Skylab to mission control. "Hello, Houston. This is Skylab. Are you reading me?" The ear-pleasing conversation continued, stunning the mission controllers, until the hoax was exposed: Astronaut Owen Garriott had recorded the conversation during a private communications session with his wife, Helen.

Then the time came to close up shop again. After 59 days in orbit, on September 25, 1973, at 6:20 P.M., eastern daylight time, the Command Module splashed down in the Pacific Ocean. The 24-million-mile mission ended only six seconds from the predicted time, and the astronauts were quickly hoisted aboard the U.S.S. *New Orleans*. They were a bit wobbly as they stepped onto the carrier's deck, but despite their longer time in orbit, they were in better shape than the first crew. Effects on their bodies of zero-gravity living appeared to have stabilized by the 40th day. Alan Bean had lost the most weight, about 8½ pounds. There was some deterioration in muscle tone of all the men, but a vigorous exercise program had kept their condition at a generally high level, and all felt they could have remained in space much longer.

So the second Skylab mission was over. It had, among other things, dispelled many fears of long-duration spaceflight. And now the scientists and engineers have their work cut out for them for years to come, digesting the data gathered during these two months. There were no speeches this day. The Navy band only played a one-minute salute. Return from space had become routine. But—that was what NASA was striving for.

Troubles continued to plague Skylab to the last. Days before launch of the third crew, a routine inspection revealed cracks in stabilization fins on the Saturn 1 B, which would carry the men into orbit. Launch was delayed until the fins could be removed and replaced.

The Final Mission

With 28- and 59-day Skylab missions under its belt, NASA wanted to take another big step in spaceflight duration, up to 85 days. The extension was prompted not only by the wish to gather additional information on prolonged flight but also to get an extraterrestrial look at the comet Kohoutek, the "comet of the century." The launch of the third crew, SL-4 in NASA terminology, was set back a month so as to coincide with Kohoutek's passage within view of the earth. Before the final mission could be launched, however, problems had to be solved on the ground.

On October 23, 1973, the fuel tanks of the first stage of the Saturn IB were filled with fuel during a test exercise and then allowed to vent. It was raining at the time, and technicians neglected to remove plastic covers on inlets that allowed pressures inside the tanks to equalize with atmospheric pressure. The thin domes of two of the tanks were sucked in by the lower pressure inside the tanks, and the mission was in jeopardy. Fortunately, by slowly filling the tanks with fuel and helium gas, technicians were able to remove the "dimples," and the mission was "go" again.

Then on November 10, just five days before launch, another glitch occurred. Fourteen hairline cracks were found on the eight fins that supported the 1.3-million-pound Saturn IB on the pad and would guide its flight immediately after lift-off. Engineers feared the cracks would expand with the stresses of launch, causing the fins to break off, possibly leading to catastrophic failure of the giant bird. Launch was delayed five days while new fins were installed. And still SL-4 was not ready to go. More cracks were found, this time in the structure between the Saturn's first and second stages. Launch was delayed another day. But then engineers decided the cracks would not endanger the crew, and the final countdown began, climaxing in a nominal launch on November 16. Eight hours later, on their third attempt, the three rookie astronauts docked the Command/Service Module with Skylab.

To prevent the motion sickness that afflicted the second crew, astronauts Gerald Carr, Edward Gibson, and William Pogue took special medication, spent the first night in space in the CSM, and completed activation of the laboratory at a cautious and deliberate pace. The men had also flown aerobatic maneuvers in T-38 jets the day before lift-off, and Dr. Gibson had worked underwater to further increase his tolerance. The cautionary measures seemed to work. Of the three, only Bill Pogue suffered from a bit of sickness and coughed up a mouthful of vomit. The men talked about covering up Pogue's illness by dropping the "barf bag" into the trash receptacle. However, their conversations were accidentally transmitted to earth. The result: A friendly "chewing out" by Alan Shepard, chief of the astronaut office of the Johnson Space Center, for trying to hide a potential medical problem.

Skylab's food supply was sufficient only for an additional 70-day mission. Thus, the third crew carried special food supplements into orbit, 392 bars—vanilla, chocolate, and strawberry, with chocolate chip, crispy, or flaky centers. The cookies—each 2 inches by 4 inches, weighing almost 2 ounces, and providing 300 calories each—were eaten every third day to stretch the food supply. The men also carried with them 75 pounds of regular Skylab food, plus another 25 pounds of high-calorie chocolate bars. In all, the food supply was expanded for an 85-day mission, plus an additional 10 days in case of emergency.

The crew spent Thanksgiving, Christmas, and New Year's Day in orbit. The highlight of Thanksgiving Day was a record-setting space walk. This, like so many of Skylab's activities, was not without its minor difficulties. Garments similar to long johns worn under the space suits had become damp and mildewed between missions. The men sprayed them with disinfectant and spread them out like athletic uniforms around the Orbital Workshop. The garments dried overnight and were ready for use Thanksgiving Day. Among other jobs on their first space walk, astronauts Pogue and Gibson had the difficult task of repairing a radar antenna. The two men spent 6 hours, 37 minutes, and 37 seconds outside the laboratory—breaking the record set by the second crew only a few months earlier. After the walk outside, the trio "sat down" to Thanksgiving dinner.

The men spent a rather lonely Christmas. To cheer them, Yuletide carols were broadcast from mission control, and the men made and decorated a Christmas tree from odds and ends aboard the station. On this day Carr and Pogue stepped outside for a record-setting 7-hour-plus-one-minute space walk. While outside, they took numerous pictures of the comet Kohoutek as it made a near pass to the sun. These and other photographs from Skylab's unique vantage point—free of the earth's atmosphere—will probably turn out to be the best

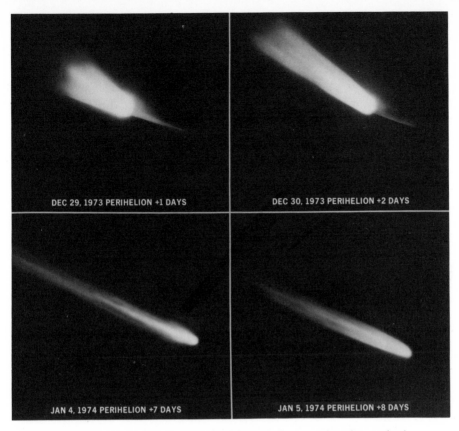

DEC 29, 1973 PERIHELION +1 DAYS

DEC 30, 1973 PERIHELION +2 DAYS

JAN 4, 1974 PERIHELION +7 DAYS

JAN 5, 1974 PERIHELION +8 DAYS

Realistic drawings of the elusive comet Kohoutek, by an artist who worked from the astronauts' sketches and descriptions.

ever taken of the so-called Christmas comet. Heralded months in advance as likely to outclass Halley's comet of 1910, Kohoutek never achieved its predicted brilliance. It approached the earth, passed it, and unobtrusively slipped away into space—a vast disappointment to the millions of people who vainly searched the skies.

The astronauts rounded out the holiday season by celebrating the new year 16 times as they circled earth, in and out of different time zones.

Among the multitude of experiments this last crew performed was an interesting one with a thousand gypsy moth eggs. On earth, sterilized male moths are used to control the spread of devastation of forests by the destructive gypsy moth. On earth, hatching requires approximately six months. After about a month in orbit, the astronauts excitedly announced that they were attending physicians to the hatching of the first five of the eggs. The purpose of the experiment was to learn if weightlessness can shorten the hatching time of the moths, with the thought that in the future the sterilized males may be produced much faster when needed.

Early in the third flight a problem with one of the three control gyroscopes that maintain the station in proper orientation caused fears that the mission might have to be ended early. The gyros were critical to the maneuvering of the space station—as, for example, in rolling over to take pictures of Kohoutek or for the earth resources surveys. However, NASA engineers were able to compensate for the loss of the gyro by canceling some maneuvers, expending a little more fuel for others, and making some a little less demanding. A few weeks after the first gyroscope incident, a second gyro began acting up, and fears that the mission would have to be terminated were renewed. But even if only a single gyro were functioning, the crew would not have been in jeopardy. The men could have made a normal return or even stayed aboard for a while longer conducting limited experiments. Fortunately, serious problems with the second gyro never materialized, and the mission lasted a full 84 days.

On Friday, February 8, 1974, at 11:17 A.M., eastern daylight time, astronauts Carr, Gibson, and Pogue—space rookies no longer—splashed down in the Pacific in a landing that had become so routine that no live TV coverage took place. The Skylab adventure—many years and millions of man-hours in the making, at a cost of $2.6 billion—had come to a successful conclusion. The great laboratory, which had been placed in orbit nearly nine months earlier and had been oc-cupied and kept "alive" by three crews, was now at the mercy of the forces of gravity and of the intense heat and cold of space. It could remain in orbit up to six years or more, gradually slowing and settling toward earth. Its end will be a fiery one as it brushes with earth's atmosphere.

The future? The immediate picture is international. In 1975, a Soyuz manned spacecraft will be launched from the Soviet Union. Shortly thereafter an Apollo Command/Service Module essentially like those used in the Skylab mission will be launched from Cape Kennedy. The two crafts will hook up in orbit. The docking system—which may be used at some future date to rescue each other's space-men if they get into difficulty—will be tested. In addition, the crews will be exchanged and experiments performed.

And beyond? There is the space shuttle, a manned two-stage launch vehicle. Since both stages of each launch will be recovered and re-used many times, each launch will cost significantly less than any-thing now possible. In the future, probably during the 1980s, the shuttle may be used to assemble and equip a permanent space station capable of housing dozens of men.

Skylab! Man more than flexed his space muscles with Skylab. He put those muscles to work. He used his technology. And he built a doorway into the future.

Index

Acknowledgments

Special acknowledgment for assistance in the preparation of this book goes to Mr. Mitchell Sharpe, Manned Flight Awareness Office, Marshall Space Flight Center, Huntsville, Alabama; Mr. Joe Jones, Public Affairs Office, Marshall Space Flight Center, Huntsville, Alabama; and the Public Affairs Offices of NASA Headquarters, Washington, D.C., the Kennedy Space Center, Cape Kennedy, Florida, and the Lyndon B. Johnson Space Center, Houston, Texas.

About the Authors

William G. Holder

An aerospace engineer for the U.S. Air Force and an active free-lance writer, William G. Holder is able to translate his highly technical scientific knowledge into terms comprehensible to the layman. Author of a book on Saturn V as well as of numerous articles related to the space program, Mr. Holder began his writing career in his youth as a sports reporter for the *Cincinnati Inquirer*. Although he continued to be an avid sports fan, his interests, since college, have centered around aerospace engineering. Mr. Holder's enthusiasm for the Skylab space mission stems from his belief that it will benefit people all over the world. "The Skylab program marks a major change in direction for the U.S. space program—a direction that will aid the people of the earth in years to come," he says. "Instead of landing on the moon and looking back at earth from a distance of a quarter of a million miles, we will view the earth from a unique position only 235 nautical miles away. This change of viewpoint should give us a decidedly different picture of our world."

Major William D. Siuru, Jr., USAF

A career officer in the U.S. Air Force, Major William D. Siuru, Jr., has been involved with either advanced airplanes or space vehicles since his graduation from college. He has a master's degree in aeronautical engineering from the Air Force Institute of Technology and is currently doing research for his doctorate at Arizona State University. Author of several articles on airplanes, automobiles, and spacecraft, he has contributed to both popular and scientific publications. Now, in collaboration with William Holder, Major Siuru turns his attention to what he considers one of the most exciting events in the history of manned spaceflight. "Skylab has tested and proved man's ability to adapt to and solve unexpected problems in space," he says. "Demonstrating great ingenuity and working essentially from scratch, space scientists designed, in a matter of days, hardware that enabled them to save what could have been a dismal space failure. In the future, the repair of broken satellites will become a commonplace procedure, and today, Skylab's success marks a truly great achievement in space history."